Life under Construction

Decisions,
Decisions,
Decisions

Kenneth Raymond

To everyone seeking a better life

iUniverse, Inc.

New York   Bloomington

iUniverse books may be ordered through booksellers or by contacting:

iUniverse
1663 Liberty Drive
Bloomington, IN 47403
www.iuniverse.com
1-800-Authors (1-800-288-4677)

ISBN: 978-1-4401-9233-3 (sc)
ISBN: 978-1-4401-9235-7 (hc)
ISBN: 978-1-4401-9234-0 (ebook)

Printed in the United States of America

iUniverse rev. date: 02/26/2010

Life under Construction is in response to what has been impressed in my spirit to communicate to Christians around the world. There is a Bible verse that states that people will perish for a lack of knowledge. That is true; however, I do not think this is the number one problem facing many Christians today. I believe what holds believers back from experiencing the best that God has for them are the issues of preparation and execution. God has done well in communicating both His love and His word to us. Today, there are more capable ministers than ever before communicating the word of God. The number of Christian academies and Christian universities teaching the word of God are increasing daily all over the world. Outside of these higher institutions of learning, the programs that we receive via church, conferences, Internet, cable, satellite, print, television, and movies reach more markets and more areas of the world than ever before. Therefore, knowledge of God's word is improving and expanding; however, there remains a major issue confronting the Body of Christ today. As Christians, we are to be doers of the word and not hearers only. *James 1:22—Do not merely listen to the word, and so deceive yourselves. Do what it says (NIV).*

After we have heard the word, we need to put forth a more concerted effort in the areas of preparing ourselves for the blessings of God and in the execution of the works He wants us to accomplish for His purpose.

If the word of God can create a complex world and bring all the entities of that world together, acting as one to support life, think what could happen in our individual lives if we simply acted upon what He has informed us to do.

Dedication

First, I dedicate *Life under Construction* to God the Father, Jesus, and the Holy Spirit. The objective for *Life under Construction* is that it becomes a resource to help people all over the world understand their position in Christ, to enable them to achieve the quality of life Jesus died to give us. I also want to thank God for the Holy Spirit, who was instrumental in writing *Life under Construction*.

To Freda Dents, and IUniverse's Editorial Consultant Manager, Sarah Disbrow. Thank you for your dedication to this project. Your work and helpful insights were critically important to *Life under Construction*. Thank you again for your contributions.

To pastors Rex and Bobbie Gwaltney, my spiritual mentors. Thank you for your faith, strength, courage, and love. You have been an inspiration and great role models to thousands of people around the world. May God continue to bless you richly for your labor of love in Christ. To my wife Pennie and daughter E. Nicole, thank you for your endless support and love. Both of you are my Zephaniah 3:17. Finally, yet importantly, I want to thank my mother, Ann Raymond. Your children call you blessed because of your commitment and love for the family. On behalf of us all, thank you for all that you do, and may God continue to delight Himself in you for your unwavering support and personal sacrifices. We thank God for you every day.

Life under Construction is designed to address many of the issues we are confronted with on a daily basis. By accepting our assignment to follow the will of God, and to follow the kingdom examples outlined in *Life under Construction*, decision-making can be improved, and the quality of life experienced in our walk with God can reach new heights. Read well, hear what God is saying to you, be wise in His understanding, do what He says, and prosper!

3 John 1:2—Beloved, I wish above all things that thou mayest prosper and be in health, even as thy soul prospereth.

Have you ever thought, "Why did I do that?" or, "I wish I would have followed my first instincts"? Or perhaps you have said to yourself, "How could I have been so stupid!" We have all been in situations where we have said to ourselves, "I wish I knew what to do!" Life is full of decisions. We make decisions every day regarding what to buy, who to listen to, where to live, what is best for us, what is best for our children, who we should trust, what career or job to pursue, what school to attend. Do I want to remain single, or do I want to get involved again? These are only a few examples of the questions we must answer on a daily basis. *Decisions, decisions, decisions.*

Decision-making is a fact of life, and as believers we need to improve in this area. Each day brings with it issues that we have to decide how to handle. Our lives are directly or indirectly affected by the decisions we either make or do not make. The results are either positive or negative. The good news is that we can positively affect the quality of our lives by following the will (light) of God and yielding to the guidance and influence of the Holy Spirit.

Contents

Foreword by Anthony L. Johnson, PhD

For ages, fear in decision-making has been the marker between success and failure. Many dreams, gifts, and talents have been left idle due to fear, indecision, and presupposed uncertain outcomes. It is understandable that decision-making can be an arduous task because the results that surface not only impact our lives but the world around us. In many ways, decision-making cannot be avoided because life is designed from a framework of individual contributions emerging to manifest a cause. The concept of emergence is the embodiment of the Trinitarian view of God, whereas the Father, the Son, and the Holy Spirit function individually and collectively. Each exists with a unique purpose so that continuous progress and success may be constructed within the lives of humans.

Many people have searched for an understanding of life in an effort to develop the capacity to initiate decisions that will be for the greater good of their lives. Some of us contend that actions are more important than the thoughts, which often precede them. Indeed, our actions and words reveal what is important to us and where God stands in our lives. In the Bible, Acts 7 expresses how walking in step with God gives us power and wisdom so that we can overcome the limitations of a task. Therefore, decisions are in essence comprised of conceptual elements that can help us construct a successful life.

Decisions influence how we transition from one stage of life to the next. Life transitions cannot be consumed physiologically in totality but can encompass the psychological and spiritual elements as well. Decisions reflect our sense of awareness about how we view ourselves and what outcome we project within life's endeavors. To possess the confidence needed to make decisions and to access resources for effective decision-making shows our concern for our lives, our families, our friends, our business associates, and the world at large. Therefore, it becomes real that our lives are filled with purpose to influence others.

Decisions should not subject us to becoming positioned in a place of indifference. However, through the resources of God, our capacity to make effective decisions can be enhanced. Moreover, we can begin to make a difference in life. It is disheartening, however, that many spend time wavering in decision-making between natural resources and spiritual reasoning. Scripture challenges us in *1 Kings 18:21* to cease from wavering within decision-making and allow God to direct our path—*And Elijah came unto all the people, and said, how long will you waver between two opinions? If the Lord be God, follow Him.*

Decisions endorse our commitment to God, to self, and to others. All decisions, whether large or small, complex or simple, construct an edifice for our lives. The scriptures make references to decision-making, and how through God, we obtain divine insight on how our lives are constructed according to the will of God. *Romans 12:1–2—I urge you, in view of the mercies of God, to present your bodies as living sacrifices, holy and pleasing to God, which is your spiritual worship. Do not conform any longer to the pattern of this world, but be transformed by the renewing of your mind. Then you will be able to test and approve what is the good, acceptable, and perfect will of God.*

Many elements influence decision-making in life. Kenneth Raymond's book, *Life under Construction*, is a biblical landscape referencing how the decision-making process can bring our path into alignment with God's design for our lives. The significance in this writing is deep-rooted within the use of biblical illustrations referencing how God's directions serve as a resource to stimulate a person's mental faculties for effective decision-making. *Life under Construction* outlines how God's direction breathes life into a person so that spiritual insight and control can both initiate and regulate the decision-making process. Mr. Raymond is uniquely qualified to author *Life under Construction* due to his varied background related to helping individuals improve their quality of life, and his ministerial experience of more than twenty years. He is the co-founder of GTKH ministries in Southlake, Texas. Additionally, Mr. Raymond is well acquainted with the decision-making process because of his thirty-one years of experience as an executive with a Fortune 500 company. Not only was Mr. Raymond responsible for the decisions of staff managers, he also had the added responsibility of corporate and region school trainers. In these roles, Mr. Raymond fine-tuned the communication, coaching, and decision-making skills of service providers and management employees. Mr. Raymond's book, *Life under Construction*, is an educational endeavor into the wisdom of God and the inner self. It reveals how our direction in life evolves through our decisions. The hallmark of this writing highlights God's wisdom as a representation of life tools that allows us to draw upon a resource that transcends natural human capacity in our pursuit of success in life.

Decisions are daily exercises that afford us the opportunity to build our lives on a solid foundation. Over time, our lives become a construction site for knowledge, understanding, and wisdom. *Life under Construction* encourages spiritual allegiance so that each life decision will exhibit faith so that the abundance of God's blessings can be experienced. *Life under Construction* will help you formalize your commitment to God so that your decision-making will represent God's model of faithfulness, obedience, holiness, and righteousness. All Christians and seekers who desire to enhance their ability to exercise faith within life's decisions in an effectual manner should take advantage of this resource. *Life under Construction* will help strengthen your inner resolve so that you may overcome the influences that can hinder effective decision-making and stagnate your progression. Thus, your decisions can represent the infallible truth of God. *Life under Construction* seeks to open your mind so that the wisdom of God can become your resource for constructing

a life of decisions that produce success.

Anthony L. Johnson, PhD

author of *To Be Determined*

Director, Growing Through Life Experiences, Inc.

Chapter One
The Mind of the Creator

God is the author and owner of our beautiful universe, the Creator of all first-born visible things. What He thinks He creates, and the things He creates are very good. In the beginning, God conceived in His mind a world that He would create. He envisioned all the things He would place within His world, that is, how it would function and the design of the man to whom He would give the responsibility for maintaining portions of the creation. As we read the account of the creation in the first chapter of Genesis, notice how each particular day was established upon the previous day. God evaluated each stage of His creation and pronounced it very good.

Genesis 1:31—And God saw everything that He had made, and, behold, it was very good. And the evening and the morning were the sixth day.

In Genesis 1:31, God was simply validating His creation in relationship to how it was predetermined in His mind to look and

1

function! Incrementally, stage by stage, God moved forward until the creation was completed. God's creation had six developmental stages, completed over a course of six days. Each stage was strategically planned to build upon the previous stage. Man entered upon the scene last because everything that needed to be made had been made. The creation was now ready to be managed for God by the man He created. That man was Adam.

We can learn a valuable lesson from the creation process; it represents how God operates. God releases to us things according to His timing. Our lack of patience will not push God into moving out of sequence. We also learn that we are specifically created and prepared by God to handle responsibility. Each blessing that God gives us has to be responded to in a dependable way! We see an example of this with Adam in the garden and in reading how Joshua fulfilled the command of God as he prepared to enter the promised land. You will note that Joshua did not possess all the land of Canaan at one time. As the nation of Israel was prepared to handle the battles and occupy the land strategically, God allowed them to move forward progressively. Otherwise, they would have been overwhelmed by the situation, or, as the Bible states, eaten up by the land and its inhabitants. The flow of things from God to us will follow this same pattern. They will come gradually and build upon one another until the process is complete. Stages of development will take time. We have to walk with God, learning from Him and building competency as we follow His plan. When the time is right, God will release good things to us! God is a strategic thinker. He strategizes how He is going to position the believer to receive the blessed thing. Once the individual is ready, God puts His plan in motion and prepares the individual according to the level of responsibility he or she is designed to handle.

To illustrate further what God does in creation, we will substitute the word *company* for the word *creation*. In the mind of the company executives, the goal is to create a product that will achieve an expected end. The company that produces the product is only pleased when the product fulfills its purpose. With the Father, Jesus made everything on the earth to interact and function in a harmonious manner. After the sixth day, the Father's creation was fulfilling its purpose. Adam was created and placed in the Garden of Eden—the earth. According to God's purpose, Adam and the Garden of Eden were designed to function together harmoniously. Eden would produce, and Adam would manage. In placing Adam in the Garden of Eden, God understood that Adam would be confronted with situations that would require him to make decisions, including the influence of Lucifer. Therefore, Adam was specifically designed with the intelligence and spiritual ability to function in the environment God created for him. With this ability, Adam was empowered to accomplish the will of God. To help Adam, God walked with him and instructed him in how to manage his environment and how to live a productive and peace-filled life. However, Adam's peaceful condition turned into an evil, stress-filled situation when he disobeyed God. Because of Adam's decision to sin, the product he was designed to govern for God was taken over and controlled by Satan. God's will was for Adam to have control, not Satan. God was not surprised by this event. God is all-knowing. He knows the end from the beginning. He knew the fall of man would happen based upon a decision not to follow His word—the "company's manual."

God had given Adam specific instructions not to eat of the fruit of the Tree of the Knowledge of Good and Evil. To ensure that Adam knew what to do, God discussed with him daily the things he had to do so that his environment would produce what it was designed to produce. God was Adam's personal coach and counselor, motivating and training him. Adam's ability was God given. Complying with the temptation of Satan was something Adam had power over. Adam decided to disregard the company's instructions and he forfeited his right of ownership. The valuable lesson we learn from Adam's mistake is that we must discipline ourselves to keep the things God gives us. In order to receive the benefits of ownership, the owner's instructions must be followed when the things of God are placed in our hands. It is far more convenient to hold onto the things of God when we receive them initially than to try and recover them at a later time.

God's original concept of man produced a spiritual, understanding man who was designed, trained, and motivated to walk after His will. God uses the Gospel of Jesus Christ to create a man with the same aspects of His original creation. As born-again Christians, we have the same strengths and tendencies as our father in the flesh Adam had. The exception with us is that we are a more empowered model because of the spiritual gifts God has given us through Jesus. The born-again believer has the personal characteristics of the model of man God is motivated to empower and train to keep the things He establishes. God will place His blessings in their hands.

The following scriptures identify what happens with the man that

makes provision to do things God's way.

Psalm 1:1–3—Blessed is the man who does not walk in the counsel of the wicked, or stand in the way of sinners, or sit in the seat of mockers. But his delight is in the law of the Lord, and on His law he meditates day and night. He is like a tree planted by streams of water, which yields its fruit in season and whose leaf does not wither. Whatever he does prospers (NIV).

This particular set of scriptures represents the character traits that

God respects. As a result of being influenced by God, the blessed man

will make preparations for God's will and not allow other influences

to direct his actions. This man delights in following the plans of

God. As a result, this man will experience the liberty God promises

in these scriptures. Psalm 1:1–3 have universal application: they

will work anywhere in the world.

God's man is devoted to doing things His way, and the Father's

motivation is to place this individual in a prosperous environment

where streams of good things run through it. Psalm 1:3 informs us

that the results of the blessed man's efforts will yield good things

during productive seasons. The success of the man is based upon preparing to live a God-centered life: making every provision and decision to follow the plan of God enthusiastically.

God is a great decision-maker, and because we are made in His image, we have the capacity to make informed decisions as well. The way that we accomplish this goal of making informed, qualified decisions is by making the commitment to walk in God's plans according to Psalm 1:1–2. If we follow the instructions of God, we will discover that we have more freedom to take care of the concerns that we have neglected. We will also have more information to draw upon to make decisions because we are focused on what is important, and we will develop the capacity to achieve more due to the benefits of God's specifically designed growth strategy for the individual He empowers.

Chapter Two
Why Flexibility Is Important

In God, we will receive blessings from the covenant He has established with us. We receive these blessings because God decided to bless us, because we decide to follow the will of God, and because we maintain an attitude of being flexible. Things will change periodically for the believer. God expects us to embrace change with the understanding that change works to increase our knowledge, build competency, and cause us to grow spiritually, and it increases our capacity to receive and manage God's created blessing. Change can be either gradual or abrupt. Anyone pursing destiny will be confronted with change. This is their rite of passage. Unless we go through preparation stages, we cannot transition through the levels God has planned for us. Preparation stages enable us to fulfill His will by handling more responsibility. To accomplish this goal, God will take us out of our comfort zone and place us in challenging situations. God uses these challenges to strengthen and edify us for His glory.

In order to enhance us according to the purpose we are to fulfill for His glory, God will orchestrate situations that will build character and the skill sets we need to possess. Developing character and skill sets are essential in order to carry out God's will. Skill sets could include faith, patience, self-esteem, communication skills, administrative skills, technical skills, leadership skills, etc. Based upon the individual's God-given function, God will place individuals in situations, such as particular careers, jobs, partnerships, schools, ministries, etc., designed to prepare them to carry out their assignment. Jacob is an excellent example of an individual who demonstrated flexibility in order to achieve his God-given function.

Through the counsel of his godly parents, Jacob relocates to the land of his father's nativity. Actually, it was God working behind the scenes directing and establishing Jacob's footsteps. It was God who "planted" Jacob in this situation. This was where God wanted Jacob to be! Ultimately, in this predetermined place, everything that Jacob touched would prosper. He would experience the streams of prosperity that Psalm 1:3 promises. Jacob's prosperity would be underwritten and guided by the providence and instructions of God.

As we read the story of Jacob, beginning in Genesis chapter 28, we see in the scriptures that Jacob worked for a wicked and unscrupulous man named Laban. Laban was a thief; he changed Jacob's wages ten times, and he misled him on numerous occasions. Because Jacob decided to do things God's way, Laban was not able to cause him to forfeit this great opportunity created by God. God was developing him into the caliber of man He needed him to become. God deliberately sent Jacob to Laban's area to build faith and wealth, to develop the patriarchal family, and to learn administrative and leadership skills. Working with Laban and living in this hostile environment was very difficult for Jacob. Because of the difficulty of the situation and the way he was treated, Jacob had reason to give up and return home. He was in this strange place, unsure of what the future held. Having only the promise from God that He was going to bless him, Jacob had to walk by faith. The only support Jacob could depend upon was from God, and at times, Jacob had lapses in his faith. Although Jacob was pressed to find a comfortable moment, quitting was not an option. God did not bring him into this environment to be defeated. This was the place where Jacob's destiny was being fulfilled, and God was going to ensure Jacob received everything he was predestined to receive! Laban's treatment of Jacob was not going to offset the plan of God.

As we see in Jacob's situation, God knows how to level the playing field and to shift it to our advantage in the environments He assigns us to. God gave strength to Jacob to do what he could not do in his own strength. Through revelation, Jacob received the ability to recover all the wages that Laban stole from him and more. In the process of God blessing Jacob, Laban's wealth also increased. However, Laban's wealth increased only because it was managed under the hands of Jacob.

Genesis 30:27—And Laban said unto him, I pray thee, if I have found favor in thine eyes, tarry: for I have learned by experience that the Lord hath blessed me for thy sake.

Finally, after cheating Jacob ten times, Laban acknowledged that God was establishing Jacob as a man of prosperity, and, consequently, he was being blessed. What was the key to Jacob's prosperity? It was a combination of two things: the first was the predetermined function for his life, and the second was preparing for God to use him according to his life's mission!

When we make provision in our lives to do things God's way, God will give us power over obstacles and give us insights that allow us to achieve good results and to move forward. In Jacob's life, Laban was a significant problem. However, God empowered Jacob through His word to have success despite Laban's tactics. Look at Genesis 31:10–12. It gives an account of Jacob meditating in the field one day. God not only gives Jacob a strategy to defeat Laban and accomplish his predetermined goal in working for Laban, God also gives him the instructions in how to accomplish the strategy.

Genesis 31:10–12—In breeding season I once had a dream in which I looked up and saw that the male goats mating with the flock were streaked, speckled, or spotted. The angel of God said to me in the dream, Jacob. I answered, here I am. And He said, look up and see that all the male goats mating with the flock are streaked, speckled, or spotted, for I have seen all that Laban has been doing to you (NIV).

This vision is a critical component in Jacob moving forward and fulfilling his destiny to become a man of real wealth. In the vision, God made known to Jacob the species of livestock that He was going to bless, the ones that would become significantly active in producing offspring because of His anointing on them. What was once inconceivable to Jacob now became visible. With this strategy, Jacob not only overcame the theft of his wages by Laban, he also moved to a higher level of responsibility in managing the blessings he received. The level of blessings Jacob began to receive from the hand of God necessitated him expanding his territory to accommodate the blessings. This is why it was important for Jacob to stay motivated and committed to God's strategy during his stay in this hostile environment. If Jacob had faltered or lost his focus and commitment, look at the size of the opportunity he would have forfeited or delayed. However, because Jacob followed the instructions of God, his livestock increased exceedingly, he developed the skill set to manage God's blessing, and he became the wealthy, influential man God needed him to become.

From the account of Jacob's story, we see that in this predetermined place, Jacob was challenged, and in the challenge, he was made stronger than he had been before. Jacob was flexible enough in his attitude to allow God to work through him and for him. Jacob maintained his focus, and he achieved God's predetermined goals for working with Laban.

Noah is another example of an individual who exercises good decision-making and is flexible with God as God controls his affairs and moves him forward in destiny. In studying Noah's life, we see a few of the same patterns God used in moving Jacob forward. Noah was a righteous man, predisposed in making preparation for God to order his footsteps. God would use Noah as He prepared to bring the floodwaters upon the earth.

In the sixth chapter of Genesis, God begins to talk to Noah about His strategy. He instructed Noah where to locate and what to preach. He also gave him the design of the ark, the type of wood to use, how to seal the ark, and where to build the ark's window and door. God also instructed Noah in the exact number and types of animals to bring into the ark. Noah's instructions were to preach, build the ark, and bring in the animals. Noah faced humiliation, ridicule, and mockery. However, he knew it was the will of God to follow these instructions. Noah made provision to fulfill all the instructions God gave him. Now it was up to God to fulfill His promise.

As Noah completed the building of the ark, God supplied the water to fulfill the purpose that Noah was to accomplish. The heavens opened, and it rained for forty days and nights. The foundations of the deep were also opened, assisting in bringing about the floodwaters upon the earth.

Genesis 7:11–12—In the six hundredth year of Noah's life, on the seventeenth day of the second month—on that day all the springs of the great deep burst forth, and the floodgates of the heavens were opened. And rain fell on the earth forty days and forty nights (NIV).

Everyone who thought Noah had lost his mind soon realized that he knew more than what they thought! God's strategy was in full effect. The ark floated right where God had instructed Noah to build it.

Where God calls us to, He will supply the needs we have, and we will build the skill sets we need to handle the responsibility He gives us. You can have confidence in your ability to make quality decisions as you follow the instructions of God's word.

Assignments chosen by God will have some level of difficulty. This is the way we are strengthened. Doing things we are not accustomed to enhances our capacities to handle greater levels of responsibilities. When assignments are chosen for us, inherent within the assignment is what we need to be prepared, blessed, and propelled forward in the timing and purposes of God. If you are currently in a challenging situation chosen by God, you are being developed and blessed. God will give you the information you need to overcome your obstacles and improve your situation. When the situation is over, you will have the brilliance that God wanted you to receive. Your responsibility is to stay focused and do what you can, and God will do the rest!

Destiny works in the life of the believer to produce strength and to accomplish the predetermined purposes of God. Each individual's destiny has its own predetermined set of goals, skill requirements, and patterns in how the individual will eventually accomplish God's desired end. If it is financial power that you are to have, God knows how to get money to you. If you are an entrepreneur, God will not only help you with your business model, He will also help you with your mission statement, your product design, and your marketing strategy. Just look at what God did for Jacob and Noah. God knows best. He knows the best location for you, your family, and your business. God has already completed the logistic studies for us. How do we receive these things? We receive these things through revelation and reflection as we walk in the plans of God. God allows us to see into the spirit realm the things He is going to manifest on the earth. It is at this point when the blessings begin to flow.

God will supply the needs we have. If we follow His will and the instructions He gives us, success is guaranteed. Psalm 1:1 states that we should refuse to go in the direction of the wicked man, no matter how great the influences are. Psalm 1:3 states that God will locate us, according to His purpose, to prosperous surroundings. In these environments, God will challenge us, help us with training, and supply the needs we have. If we follow this model today, our position becomes a blessed position that is of great value to both others and ourselves.

God expects and prepares us to make good decisions. Parents raise their children with this goal in mind. They want their children to become completely functional and effective. In this same way, God trained Adam, but Adam failed by not following the training and instructions he received from God. Therefore, his relatively simple yet peaceful existence turned into a nightmare. God gave Adam the power to make decisions. He directed him in how to maintain the success He had given him. God watched Adam operating in the garden and approved of his decisions. Jesus followed the same principles with His disciples, training and building faith in them until they were ready to become fishers of men. Adam understood God's ways, conducted himself accordingly, and received the benefits of his environment, until he disobeyed the instructions of God. Adam gambled away his guarantee on a careless decision. That decision had devastating results.

Believers have to remain diligent and faithful to what they receive from God. There is great value in documenting what God says to us, in meditating on His word, allowing the Holy Spirit to do His work in us and for us, and in seeking God's will when making decisions. Prosperity comes as a result of doing things God's way. Control of internal and external negative influences that are contrary to God's word is necessary.

2 Corinthians 10:5—We demolish arguments and every pretension that sets itself up against the knowledge of God, and we take captive every thought to make it obedient to Christ(NIV).

According to 2 Corinthians 10:5, we take authority over our thoughts so that we are not pulled off of God's plan. Nothing can take the place of being where God wants you to be, doing what God wants you to do, and being fully committed to the strategies of God. By maintaining focus and commitment to the process, the capacity to make appropriate decisions based upon God's instructions and purpose is achieved. Once you make the correct choices, God will keep His promise. The results will be good!

Chapter Three
Seeking God's Will

1 Corinthians 13:11—When I was a child, I talked like a child, I thought like a child, I reasoned like a child. When I became a man, I put childish ways behind me (NIV).

Like Adam, we have a soul: emotions, a will, and an intellect. The life of our immortal soul comes from the breath of God. God breathed into humanity, and we became a life. We received our physical nature—our anatomy—when God formed us out of the dust of the ground. This fleshly contour is the image God wanted us to have. Thus, God created a thoroughly functional being with physical abilities, and emotional and intellectual capabilities.

The will that God has given us exists at the time of our natural birth. It becomes more prominent as we grow older. As 1 Corinthians 13:11 illustrates, we have childish thoughts and inclinations through our adolescent years. As we enter into our adult years, we have to make a conscious decision to respond to things in a mature manner.

The juvenile, immature ideas, desires, and actions of the adolescent years have to be replaced with the thoughtful, accountable actions of a mature adult. As 1 Corinthians 13:11 states, there is a point in life when we have to take control over childish inclinations and respond to situations with spiritual maturity and a mature consciousness. The goal for the born-again believer is to develop his or her will in accordance with the statutes and desires of God. As mature believers, we understand that we must use our spiritual strength to control and direct our natural circumstances.

Romans 8:9—You, however, are controlled not by the sinful nature but by the Spirit, if the Spirit of God lives in you. And if anyone does not have the Spirit of Christ, he does not belong to Christ (NIV).

As a result of our conversion into the kingdom of God, we receive the power of the Holy Spirit and the objectives of God the Father. This is because we become a son of the Father and are taught that we have a responsibility to God, family, and society. Our new source of power and objectives helps us with direction and control over the old man and our natural desires. This new birth power is an active force, scrutinizing and directing our actions toward the righteousness of God. The Spirit of God we receive in the new birth is the "Pneumatikos," commonly referred to as the Holy Ghost or

Holy Spirit. The Holy Spirit is not human. He is nonnatural and nonphysical. This Spirit of God is divine. He is sent by Jesus to live inside of us, and He is not subject to the devices nor confusion of man or Satan. The Spirit of God becomes our personal leader, communicating to us so that we can understand the things of God and walk in light. This Spirit of God is intelligent. He gives us wisdom and clarity, and motivates us to follow the will of God. The Holy Spirit also gives us the awareness when to avoid negative situations. The Holy Spirit helps us achieve success as it pertains to ministry and our personal lives. As believers, we are to allow the Holy Spirit to have full recourse in our lives and over our decision-making. There are reasons why we need to allow the Holy Spirit to have complete authority over our actions.

Frequently we receive instructions from God to go to a specific place or to do a specific thing. The problem arises when our desire (will) is not in alignment with God's directions. We see numerous examples in the Bible where individuals lived according to God's plan and where they did not. We see the results those decisions created. In negative situations, usually it was the power of the will that led the individual in the wrong direction. Our fleshly will is powerful! We must exercise spiritual control over these natural desires in order to avoid negative experiences and delays.

Romans 8:15—For you did not receive a spirit that makes you a slave again to fear, but you received the Spirit of sonship. And by Him we cry, Abba, Father (NIV).

As a son, I have ownership rights to the things of the kingdom. As a son, I am also obligated to, instructed, and trained in the interests of my Father. The weakness of the sinful nature is addressed through the knowledge we gain of God and through the spiritual awakening resulting from receiving Jesus and the Holy Spirit. We are translated into the kingdom of God by the renewing of our minds. The interests of our mind and heart are changed because our spirit is renewed by the power of the Holy Spirit. The difference between our new interests and our old interests is due to the regeneration we experience in the Spirit and in the word of God. This is why Jesus informed Nicodemus that the new birth process is necessary. In this new birth process, we receive the attitude of the Son. Moreover, the Son's attitude is to please His Father.

Philippians 2:5–8—Your attitude should be the same as that of Christ Jesus. Who, being in very nature God, did not consider equality with God something to be grasped. But made Himself nothing, taking the very nature of a servant, being made in human likeness. And being found in appearance as a man, He humbled Himself and became obedient to death—even death on a cross (NIV)!

Jesus is the "hallmark" of all Christian believers. We should follow the example He has given us in serving the Father. According to Philippians 2:8, Jesus knew that His ultimate task was to die on the cross for our sins. He knew this was the will of God and that it was one of the reasons for His reincarnation in the flesh. Jesus fully embraced this as a part of His mission while here on earth. His attitude was to obey the will of the Father even though He was in the God class as the Son of God. In a covenant relationship, we follow the guidelines of that covenant based upon the commitments of the relationship. Fulfilling the commitments of the relationship has little to do with how we feel. It is more about what we agreed to do. In our covenant relationship with God, we have to do what we have committed to do, based upon our relationship with Him.

Jesus did not use His status as God the Son to escape performing the will of the Father. Faced with the imminent reality of the cross, Jesus began to experience a struggle with His fleshly desires. His fleshly desires struggled with His spiritual desire and goal to please the Father. Jesus gained control over the fleshly desire as He prayed in the Garden of Gethsemane for the will of the Father to be done. After His prayer,

Jesus received the power to submit His will to the will of the Father.

Luke 22:42—Father, if You are willing, take this cup from Me; yet not My will, but Yours be done (NIV).

Obviously, this situation was an intense emotional strain for Jesus,

and He sought the Father for strength. This example should be our

pattern of living as well when we are tempted with wrong thinking

and in times of difficulty. In seeking spiritual help, we receive power

from the Holy Spirit. In the following scriptures, Jesus informs us of

the importance of prayer to avoid temptation. Temptations can cause

delays, problems, and distractions.

Luke 22:43–46—An angel from heaven appeared to Him and strengthened Him. And being in anguish, He prayed more earnestly, and His sweat was like drops of blood falling to the ground. When He rose from prayer and went back to the disciples, He found them asleep, exhausted from sorrow. Why are you sleeping? He asked them. Get up and pray so that you will not fall into temptation (NIV).

In prayer, we are attended to by the spiritual gifts the Father has

made available to us. We receive strength from God in numerous

ways. Here, we see Jesus attended to by an angel. We do not have to

dwell in weakness, fear, and confusion. Prayer is a tool that keeps us on track. It strengthens our resolve to submit to the will of God.

Submission is obedience, and obedience is learned behavior.

Philippians 2:8—And being found in appearance as a man, He humbled Himself, and became obedient unto death, even the death of the cross (NIV).

The Godhead—Father, Son, and Holy Spirit—directs believers to obedience. This is the Father's way of ensuring that we have everything we need and more.

In Luke the second chapter, Luke tells the story about Jesus when He was twelve years old in the temple reasoning and asking questions of the scholars of His time. When His parents discovered that He was not with them on their return trip home, they returned to Jerusalem looking for Him. After three days, they discovered Jesus in the temple. As a result of His action, the scripture says that Jesus had to learn to subject Himself to the will of His parents.

Luke 2:51—And He went down with them, and came to Nazareth, and was subject unto them. But his mother treasured all these things in her heart (NIV).

Again, Jesus is the hallmark example in how we should serve the Father. The Father will exercise His authority over our life. The Spirit of the Father will speak to us at different times and in different situations, instructing us to be obedient to His will. We have to learn to submit ourselves to the plan of God according to His will, not ours.

Proverbs 3:1—My son, forget not My law; but let thine heart keep My commandments.

A critical component that Proverbs 3:1 addresses is the condition of the heart. Within the human soul, the most powerful element is the heart. God gives us instructions to guard it carefully.

Proverbs 4:23—Keep thy heart with all diligence; for out of it are the issues of life.

The heart represents the hidden person, the part of humanity that God breathed into man, the being that cannot be seen with the naked eye. Man, through the actions of the person, only observes the personality of a man. The heart is the vitality center of a human: the center of thoughts, desires, and feelings. This hidden person of the inner man determines our disposition, and it affects our attitude. With our heart we believe, and our conscious awakening is exposed. With our mouth, we reveal the values that we are controlled by. Our behavior, then, is driven by the thoughts and emotions of the heart. Because of the power of the heart, God shifted His focus from the external, ceremonial activities of the Old Testament to our innermost being in the New Testament.

Jeremiah 31:32–33—Not according to the covenant, which I made with their fathers in the day when I took them by the hand to bring them out of the land of Egypt, My covenant which they broke, although I was their Husband, says the Lord. But this is the covenant which I will make with the house of Israel. After those days, says the Lord, I will put My law within them, and on their hearts will I write it; and I will be their God, and they will be My people (AMP).

God wants to control our natural temperament with His spiritual power. The Holy Spirit's compulsion is to communicate the love and will of God into the heart of man so that each person has the power to control his or her will.

Romans 8:1–11—Those who belong to Christ Jesus are no longer under God's sentence. I am now controlled by the law of the Holy Spirit. That law gives me life because of what Christ Jesus has done. It has set me free from the law of sin that brings death. The written law was made weak by our sinful nature. But God did what the written law could not do. He made his Son to be like those who have a sinful nature. He sent Him to be an offering for sin. In that way, He judged sin in His Son's human body. Now we can do everything the law requires. Our sinful nature no longer controls the way we live. The Holy Spirit now controls the way we live. Do not live under the control of your sinful nature. If you do, you will think about what your sinful nature wants. Live under the control of the Holy Spirit. If you do, you will think about what the Spirit wants. The way a sinful person thinks leads to death. But the mind controlled by the Spirit brings life and peace. The sinful mind is at war with God. It does not obey God's law. It cannot. Those who are controlled by their sinful nature cannot please God. But your sinful nature does not control you. The Holy Spirit controls you. The Spirit of God lives in you. Anyone who does not have the Spirit of Christ does not belong to Christ. Christ lives in you. So, your body is dead because of sin. But your spirit is alive because you have been made right with God. The Spirit of the One who raised Jesus from the dead is living in you. So, the God who raised Christ from the dead will also give life to your bodies, which are going to die. He will do this by the power of His Spirit, who lives in you (NIrV).

The Spirit of God is the wellspring of life. It brings with itself an active word that directs the activities of the man. The responsibility of humanity is to allow the Spirit and word to flow in their heart unabridged, without restraint, producing the behavior that is pleasing to God. This experience is like the bridle in a horse's mouth. It becomes a controlling factor in our lives. We must guard what we allow into our heart. For this reason, God directs us to allow the knowledge of His will and other spiritual influences to dwell in our heart.

Ephesians 5:17–19—Wherefore, be ye not unwise, but understanding what the will of the Lord is. And be not drunk with wine, wherein is excess; but be filled with the Spirit; Speaking to yourselves in psalms and hymns and spiritual songs, singing and making melody in your heart to the Lord.

Understanding the power of the heart in the life of the believer is an important issue. A faithful illustration used in biblical circles is the story of a young eagle raised by a chicken. High above a chicken farm, a mother eagle laid an egg in her nest. One day, a storm blew through the mountains where the eagle's nest rested. The nest was caught up in a zephyr of wind and, miraculously, landed in the chicken yard below. After some time a mother hen noticed the egg. She adopted the egg as one of her own. Not many days later, a baby eagle was born into the mother hen's family. Immediately, the mother hen recognized that there was something different about this "chicken." The mother hen continued raising this odd chicken as she did her other chicks. One day as the mother eagle was flying over the chicken compound, she heard a wonderfully familiar sound, the sound of the young eagle's voice. Curious as to what was happening and where the sound was emanating from, the mother eagle followed the sound until she discovered the young eagle walking with the chickens in the chicken compound. With a mother's intuition, the mother eagle noticed something very peculiar about this young eagle and the way it was functioning in the compound. The mother eagle decided to get a closer look at the situation and the young eagle. As the mother eagle landed within inches of the young eagle, looking intensely into his eyes, the young eagle became very nervous. The mother eagle noticed the development of the stature of the young eagle, particularly his wings. The mother eagle began to display the wide expanse of her wings to the young eagle. The mother eagle did this a number of times, coaxing the young eagle to do the same thing. At this time, the mother eagle noticed the father of the young eagle soaring overhead. Again, the mother eagle began displaying her wings and screeching at the top of her voice. The father eagle had landed within a few feet of the mother eagle and the young eagle. As the young eagle, mother eagle, and father eagle watched and circled each other on the compound, a strange dynamic occurred. The young eagle began to understand the sounds of the mother eagle, unlike the understanding he had for the mother hen. Within him, he felt the presence of another force, a pride that he had never experienced before. As the mother eagle's eyes burned into the soul of the young eagle, his fear was replaced with a sense of power and belonging. The father eagle launched himself into the air and began to soar high above the chicken farm. As the young eagle's eyes, which followed the flight of the father eagle, rested back on the eyes of the mother eagle, the mother eagle displayed her vast wingspan. This time the mother eagle, with one leap, was airborne. The young eagle, absorbed in the moment, from somewhere deep in the recesses of his heart, took courage and began to fly. He had attempted to do this before, flying only a few feet. In the past, the young eagle flew in the chicken yard when he perceived that there was danger in the yard. In an attempt to escape danger, just as many of the chickens in the yard did, he ran, jumped, and became airborne for a moment. Each time, however, the young eagle flew higher, longer, and with less effort than the chickens.

With the image in his heart changed into what he was created to be, the young eagle soared higher than he ever had before. With the young eagle back in his natural environment, he learned the natural ways of an eagle.

Isaiah 40:31—But those who hope in the Lord will renew their strength. They will soar on wings like eagles; they will run and not grow weary, they will walk and not be faint (NIV).

This illustration of the eagle serves to give insight into the power of a converted heart. It not only changes the lives of others and influences them in positive ways, but the power of the heart also has a tremendously positive effect on the person's will. The heart is the seat of the emotions. As believers, we must exercise control over our emotions. Christian counselors point to the fact that controlling one's emotions is a critical key in establishing strong relationships, having a balanced life, accomplishing life goals, and improving self-esteem. When emotions run high, if the right emotions are not engaged, mistakes can be made. We benefit from the wise and faithful heart God influences. It causes us to soar in freedom like the young eagle. With the power of God, we can accomplish anything. The responsibility that comes with His power is that we use it to glorify Him and advance His purpose. God, as the young eagle's mother did with her son, touches our heart so that we become valuable assets in the kingdom.

Another aspect of the heart is that we must fill it with encouragement. Encouragement to our heart is like blood to the body; it gives life. To avoid missing opportunities to be blessed by God, we have to learn to control our heart through encouragement. Encouragement comes in three forms: external encouragement, self-encouragement, and the encouragement that God conveys upon us directly for strength, inspiration, and direction.

In 2 Kings, the fifth chapter, we have the story of Naaman's battle with his will and the will of God. Naaman was a mighty warrior, and he is a great example of a person who struggled with God's will because he was strong, confident, and unconcerned about the will of God. In this story, Naaman is in a situation where he has no recourse but to seek God to be healed of a deadly disease.

2 Kings 5:9–11—So Naaman came with his horses and with his chariot, and stood at the door of the house of Elisha. And Elisha sent a messenger unto him, saying, go and wash in Jordan seven times, and thy flesh shall come again to thee, and thou shalt be clean. But Naaman was wroth, and went away, and said, behold, I thought, he will surely come out to me, and stand, and call on the name of the Lord his God, and strike his hand over the place, and recover the leper.

Naaman was a very proud and strong man. He accomplished many notable military victories for his king and his country. However, as we see from the scriptures, Naaman was a leper. Moreover, if he was to continue to live, God would have to heal him. Because he was a strong-willed individual, it was difficult for Naaman to submit to anything not to his liking or to his way of thinking. In the situation the scriptures describe, Naaman was tempted to not follow the will of God because he thought there was a better way to receive his healing. Naaman's will almost caused him to miss a perfect opportunity to be healed by the power of God. However, with a little encouragement, Naaman was able to overcome his will and see the value of submitting to the ways of God.

2 Kings 5:13–14—And his servants came near, and spake unto him, and said, my father, if the prophet had bid thee do some great thing, wouldest thou not have done it? How much rather then, when he saith to thee, wash, and be clean? Then went he down, and dipped himself seven times in Jordan, according to the saying of the man of God: and his flesh came again like unto the flesh of a little child, and he was clean.

In hearing his servants' encouragement and reasoning, Naaman submitted to the instructions of the prophet. Naaman repented of the way he was thinking and pursued the word of the prophet, expecting to recover from his leprosy. Naaman received the richness of the prophet's word and completely recovered from his deadly disease.

How many little "foxes" such as stubbornness and pride do we allow to hinder the blessings of God from entering into our lives? It is useless to try to change the will of God. God's decisions are always the best and accomplish the greatest good for us. God is absolute, sovereign, righteous, and infallible. He knows exactly what will work in every situation. Even with this understanding of God, at times we struggle with His will. Ultimately, we come to the understanding that it is in our best interest to do things God's way. During these times, we need encouragement and godly reasoning. Thank God for those individuals who have spoken the words of life to us, the encouragers that have assisted us in obtaining the blessing that God wanted us to have.

An example of self-encouragement is seen vividly when King David was distressed over a life-and-death situation.

1 Samuel 30:6—And David was greatly distressed, for the people spoke of stoning him, because the soul of all the people was grieved, every man for his sons and his daughters: but David encouraged himself in the Lord his God.

After returning home from battle, David discovers his home and the homes of his men burned and their families taken away by their enemies. Overwhelmed with grief, David's men thought of stoning him. David was very discouraged. With his men thinking of killing him and his wives and children taken away, David had to encourage himself in the Lord.

David exercised his faith in the goodness of God and in the strength of God's ability. One would think David remembered the battles that God had brought him through, the charity he had given to others in providing protection to them, and the promises God had given him regarding being victorious over his enemies.

1 Samuel 25:29–30—Even though someone is pursuing you to take your life, the life of my master will be bound securely in the bundle of the living by the Lord your God. But the lives of your enemies He will hurl away as from the pocket of a sling. When the Lord has done for my master every good thing He promised concerning him and has appointed him leader over Israel (NIV).

In recalling the great things God had performed in his life and the promises He had given him, David was strengthened in his faith. David learned by experience to seek the Lord for strength when situations were too difficult for him to handle.

1 Samuel 30:7–8—And David said to Abiathar the priest, Ahimelech's son, I pray thee, bring me thither the ephod. And Abiathar brought thither the ephod to David. And David inquired of the Lord saying, shall I pursue after this troop? Shall I overtake them? And He answered him, Pursue: for thou shalt surely overtake them and without fail recover all.

Like David, when we are overwhelmed by the circumstances of life, when it does not appear the goodness of God is moving, and the pure blackness of despair is all around us, God will comfort us and give us words of peace as we make our need known to Him. The presence of God and His comforting Spirit in times of trouble are indispensable. When we are full of despair, confusion, frustration, and stress, we experience a release when the Holy Spirit attends to our prayers. It is comforting to know that when we humble ourselves and seek the face of God, we can connect with His Spirit and begin the healing process.

Philippians 4:7—And the peace of God, which transcends all understanding, will guard your hearts and your minds in Christ Jesus (NIV).

We should have confidence that God will always help us regardless of the situation. He is moved by compassion toward us when we are overwhelmed by situations. He takes great pleasure when we seek Him in faith. We encourage ourselves when we think of the excellence of the power of God that can be released to help us. As we look back to 1 Samuel 30:8, we see that God releases to David exactly what he prayed for: to pursue, to overtake, and to recover all. Assured that God was for him and that his success was guaranteed, David had a spiritual revival. With his discouragement replaced with confidence and his faith renewed, David pursued the enemy and accomplished everything he mentioned in prayer. When you pray, believe that you will receive, and God will give you the desires of your heart.

Matthew 21:22— If you believe, you will receive whatever you ask for in prayer (NIV).

We should not depend upon the temporal things of this world. They are subject to change according to the power and will of God. Faith is the substance of things we hope for, the evidence of things we expect to see. God is greater and bigger than any problem or situation we will encounter in this world. We are mandated by the word of God to stir up the gift of faith that is in us, understanding that with God's help all things are possible. When negative things flood your mind, spirit, and faith, refresh yourself with good thoughts!

Philippians 4:8—Finally, brothers, whatever is true, whatever is noble, whatever is right, whatever is pure, whatever is lovely, whatever is admirable—if anything is excellent or praiseworthy-think about such things (NIV).

The third example of encouragement is the inspiration that comes directly from God. In Joshua 1:5–9, we see the Lord speaking to Joshua.

Joshua 1:5–9—No one will be able to stand up against you all the days of your life. As I was with Moses, so I will be with you, I will never leave you nor forsake you. Be strong and courageous, because you will lead these people to inherit the land I swore to their forefathers to give them. Be strong and very courageous. Be careful to obey all the law My servant Moses gave you; do not turn from it to the right or to the left, that you may be successful wherever you go. Do not let this Book of the Law depart from your mouth; meditate on it day and night, so that you may be careful to do everything written in it. Then you will be prosperous and successful. Have I not commanded you, be strong and courageous? Do not be terrified; do not be discouraged, for the Lord your God will be with you wherever you go (NIV).

Joshua was a man noted for his faith. According to Numbers 14:6, he was one of two individuals who encouraged the children of Israel to go up at once after the exodus from Egypt and possess the land of Canaan. Forty years later, as the successor to Moses, Joshua was leading Israel into battle to possess Canaan. At this time, Joshua was not completely comfortable in his ability to complete the assignment. As Joshua looked for inspiration, strength, and direction, God answered him with words of power. Three times God commanded Joshua to be strong and of a good courage. The words captured in Joshua 1:5–9 are words we should have in a prominent place: bulletin board, refrigerator, or computer screen. Because they are so powerful and speak to the very core of our faith, we should rehearse these words to ourselves daily. They remind us of the favor we have with the Father, and that man cannot stop us from receiving the blessing God wants to give us.

We all need various types of encouragements as we seek to do God's will. We need encouragement with difficult decisions and with uncertainty. As with Naaman, David, and Joshua, even strong individuals use encouragement to strengthen their commitment.

Build up yourself. Attending a church where the Holy Spirit is free to operate is tremendously important. He will help your faith develop to the level it needs to be. Strengthen the strengths God has given you. Build upon the confidence God has given you. A regular routine of fasting and prayer will play a considerable role in our spiritual life as well.

Find the resources you need to keep yourself encouraged. Do not allow the lack of encouragement to quench the passion of your heart's desire that God has given you: the ambition to seek to fulfill your destiny.

Chapter Four
Role of the Encourager

From a practical perspective, men have to become more of a central figure in the role of encourager in the family unit. In the Hebrew language, encourager means to strengthen, to fortify, or to confirm. As men, we have to be there for our children to help them through difficult times, to help them with their decision-making, to enhance their self-esteem, to give them confidence in their abilities, and with discipline. Our father in the faith, Abraham, pleased God with his reputation of being an encourager.

Genesis 18:19—For I know him, that he will command his children and his household after him, and they shall keep the way of the Lord, to do justice and judgment; that the Lord may bring upon Abraham that which He hath spoken of him.

Men not only have to transmit the love of God and His purpose to their children to encourage them in their walk with God, but they should also be encouragers from the practical perspective of training.

Training is a form of strengthening children, and the training they receive should be the best. As our father in the faith did, we must adhere to the principles Abraham followed. God expects fathers to take an active leadership role in the development of their children. As the image of strength in the family unit, fathers have a significant impact on their children. According to Ephesians 6:4, God compels men to bring their children up in the nurture and admonition of the Lord. In the Body of Christ, the role of the father in this regard is not being fulfilled in many families. Fathers should develop the type of relationship with their children that enables them to nurture their children according to their godly purpose.

Children also have to be confirmed in their identity with God. The confirmation of their faith and in their calling is more effective when it comes from someone whose opinion and leadership they have high regard for.

As the world was framed by the word of God, our lives are also framed by the words of God.

Jeremiah 1:5—Before I formed thee in the belly I knew thee; and before thou camest forth out of the womb I sanctified thee, and I ordained thee a prophet unto the nations.

The development of our life is ordained to fit within the framework God has established for each of us. God's strategic plan provides direction for our life. It directs where we are to live, who to marry—if we are to marry—the career we are to pursue, the school we are to attend, and so forth. This is called predestination. God's plan and purpose for our lives are fully developed before we arrive.

There is an order to every plan of God, and the plan is only accomplished by following the outline of the plan. An important key with predestination is that God would like His plan to be followed without exception. Obedience is better than sacrifice. Fathers should seek to eliminate all barriers preventing them from carrying out the plan of God. God understands our areas of weaknesses and works with us to improve these weaknesses.

Judges 13:12—And Manoah said, now let thy words come to pass. How shall we order the child, and how shall we do unto him?

In this scripture, we see Samson's father, Manoah, asking the angel of the Lord for directions in how to prepare his son for the purpose God was calling Samson to. The word order in the Hebrew language means to prepare, arrange, or establish. Here we see the plan of God for Samson's life unfolding to his father and mother. Manoah and his wife received directions from God in how to prepare Samson to accomplish the plans of God that lay ahead in Samson's future. God prearranged and established the conversation of Samson's two godly parents—the training and counseling they would give him, the things they would expose Samson to and discipline him in. The directions given to Samson's parents were essential in assisting them to rear their son to accomplish the divine purpose of God. God expects children to be molded in the image He has predetermined for them. Children are the Lord's heritage. As arrows in the quiver of the Lord, children have to be launched into the purpose of God's plans. Like Manoah and Samson's mother, it is the responsibility of parents to adhere to the directions God provides them to nurture and admonish their children effectively to do kingdom business.

The life of Moses offers another opportunity to illustrate the importance for parents to follow the plan of God with regard to their children's destiny. Moses had the predetermined purpose for his life to be lawgiver and to free the entire Israeli nation from Egyptian bondage. In order to prepare him to lead millions of Israelites to freedom, Moses's footsteps were prearranged by God to be reared in Pharaoh's house.

Acts 7:22—And Moses was learned in all the wisdom of the Egyptians, and was mighty in words and in deeds.

In Pharaoh's house, Moses received the training of a king. Thus, Pharaoh trained him as he would train a successor. Moses would need this training to be effective in fulfilling the plan of God. However, in his parents' home and in Jethro's tent, Moses received the spiritual training and guidance he would need to accomplish God's will. In exposing Moses to both systems of education and maturation, God was preparing Moses for the assignment to lead and govern a large and diverse group of people. Without this training, the success of Moses in accomplishing God's predetermined plans for his life would have been impeded.

Proverbs 22:6—Train up a child in the way he should go, and when he is old, he will not depart from it.

Children are greatly impacted by what they see, what they are taught, and what they hear. Children emulate their surroundings. As encouragers, parents have to walk the walk and talk the talk. James 1:22 informs us not only to be hearers of the word, but doers also. Our message to our children has to be consistent and clear. We cannot fall into the trap of expecting children to do as we say and not as we do. Actions speak louder than words, and we should not send mixed messages by what we say and what we do. Deuteronomy 6:7 represents the consistency in which we are to teach and live the word of God in the presence of our children.

Deuteronomy 6:7—You shall whet and sharpen them so as to make them penetrate, and teach and impress them diligently upon the [minds and] hearts of your children, and shall talk of them when you sit in your house and when you walk by the way, and when you lie down and when you rise up (AMP).]

What we say and do with our children should be in alignment with the will and word of God. God expects parents to be diligent with their children in teaching and training them in the plans and word of God. Our children should be "sharp" in their understanding of how God relates to their success and conduct in life.

In looking back at the words recorded in Genesis 18:19, notice that God stated that Abraham would command his whole household after him. Abraham, our father in the faith, serves as a role model in how to walk with and serve God in faith. Abraham's faithful behavior in serving God is the model we emulate today. Because Abraham walked with God and served Him with his whole heart, he could pass knowledge unto his children in how to walk with God successfully. A few of the things Abraham most likely charged his family members to observe were: govern yourself by the divine rule, walk in the statutes of the Lord because His statutes are excellent, be strong and of a good courage, and judge rightly and justly in every situation. Father God was very pleased with the position that Abraham took with his children, in commanding them to walk in righteousness.

Typically, we begin in earnest to train children in adult situations between the ages of twelve and sixteen. Most often, children are assigned domestic duties to complete. However, critical life skill components should begin early to help with this stage of transition. Two critical areas for children to gain exposure to are financial planning and integrity. Every year the level of financial debt of believers continues to increase while savings accounts and retirement funds reduce in size. There is a glut of financial debt in the Body of Christ. Money management is a significant problem for a great number of people. Money management is a national as well as an international problem. Therefore, children should understand this very important subject and get ahead of the learning curve. Children need to understand financial matters, such as leverage, borrowing, interest rates, compounding interest, tax returns, credit card debt, investing, and tithing. Children should be involved in these activities so they can understand the power of income, God's covenant, debt, and investing. As the Bible states in Ecclesiastes 10:19, money answers all things.

Another critical area for children is, or will be, the area of integrity. Societies all over the world are experiencing violations of trust in important sectors. We see breaches of trust in our financial sectors, our judicial and political systems, religious organizations, corporate institutions, and throughout educational systems. Credibility and trust will be major issues for years to come, and I am confident that most children, if not all, see breaches of integrity on a daily basis. Therefore, we can use the book of Proverbs and practical activities to educate and impress upon our children how and why it is important to be impeccable with their words and actions. We should teach them about the rewards of making plans and adhering to them, about how to complete assigned tasks on time, and about being accountable for their actions. The goal here is to make a young person's transition into the adult life as seamless and proficient as possible. Meaningful activities and exposure to effectual training will aid young people during this transitional period.

In passing the torch of the life of faith to our children, it is extremely important to communicate the course of life they have to follow.

Providing them with a picture of a person who has done it is worth a thousand words. By directing children to their predetermined paths, we actually position them to be blessed according to Psalm 1:1–3. They will experience the things of God. With this exposure and knowledge, they have a better opportunity to submit their lives to God's will.

Our highest calling as parents is to prepare our children for success, train them in biblical characteristics, and lead them by example. Children need a vision of what a godly model looks like. In the final analysis, they will look up to those who have done the will of God and pursued things in the right way, and those who give credit to God as the source of their achievement. With God's ability, children can achieve the predetermined goals God has established for them. Introduce your children to Hebrews chapter 11. Encourage them to read and study the lives of the role models they see here that were established by their faith in God.

Chapter Five
Making Decisions God's Way

Faith must be referenced when communicating biblical principles concerning what pleases God.

James 1:5–6—If any of you lack wisdom, let him ask of God, that giveth to all men liberally, and upbraideth not, and it shall be given him. But let him ask in faith, nothing wavering. For he that wavereth is like a wave of the sea driven with the wind and tossed.

We must seek God to govern our affairs wisely. Adam was the representation of the model of humanity God designed to manage the earth. In Genesis, we see that Adam was placed in the Garden of Eden, and that he was trained to make decisions. Adam's attention to the instructions of God was an indication of his ability to learn. In creating us, God gave us the ability to reason, to see the value that His word would offer us as we apply His instructions to various situations. God's wisdom in how to approach situations we are confronted with is always calculated to address a situation, problem, or crisis completely and effectively. God's answers are never wrong,

inappropriate, or ineffective. The following scriptures give us an

understanding of just how powerful and effective the wisdom of

God is.

Proverbs 8:14–16—Counsel is Mine, and sound wisdom: I am understanding: I have strength. By Me kings reign, and princes decree justice. By Me princes rule, and nobles, even all the judges of the earth.

James 1:5 says that God, out of the abundance of His heart, will

answer our questions and advise us wisely in how to handle our

problems and challenges. With confidence, we can expect special

gifts of wisdom from God. We can apply these wisdom gifts from

God to situations we encounter to gain good results and maintain

balance in life. James 1:6 is a qualifying scripture to James 1:5.

It states that, after instructions are received from God, we are not

to allow distrust to overshadow these instructions. This scripture

cautions against the lack of stability in our acceptance and faith in

God's word.

As believers, we should be firmly predisposed to follow the will

of God to remove all negative aspects of anxiety, fear, and frustration.

We are not at our best in the kingdom when we are led by anxiety,

fear, and frustration. As we see in Proverbs 8:14–16, God's word is powerful, and it will never return empty of what it promises. God's word and wisdom function as decrees in the earth. They are strong and steadfast, full of peace, justice, and prosperity. God understands that when we have peace, we are more productive, we are more creative, and we make better decisions. Thus, this is why God is actively involved and interested in our decisions.

We do not always need special gifts of wisdom to make wise decisions as we seek to control our environment and govern our affairs. God has commanded us to apply ourselves to learning, wisdom, knowledge, and understanding. God's commandment in Proverbs 4:7 informs the believer to pursue understanding in everything that we do.

Proverbs 11:14—Where no counsel is, the people fall: but in the multitude of counselors there is safety.

Proverbs 15:22—Without counsel purposes are disappointed: but in the multitude of counselors they are established.

Proverbs 11:14 states that a high-quality position for an individual is to be surrounded by able counselors. The Greek word for counselor is adviser. Advisers help with the accomplishment of God's will. The practical applications of counselors are to sharpen skills. We cannot underestimate how important this scripture is for the average individual. If we follow the guidelines of this scripture, we will maintain effective balance in our lives and develop the skills necessary to move forward progressively.

Proverbs 27:17—As iron sharpens iron, so one man sharpens another (NIV).

Here again, we have to revisit the special need for believers to be progressive in the things of God and to be committed to prepare themselves for the incredible blessings God wants to bring into their lives. Therefore, if a couple desires to engage in marriage, they should seek out wise marriage counseling. If children are to be a product of the marriage, parenting skills ought to be sought after. God requires family planning and financial planning. In the parable of the talents recorded in the twenty-fifth chapter of Matthew, the unwise steward is informed that he should have invested the money that he received so that a return on the initial investment could have been achieved. Families have to learn how to invest what God gives them.

As believers, we have to learn from the scriptures that the commitment to invest in ourselves is not a temporary situation. The commandment of God is that we are to be motivated consistently to improve our current propensity level, life skills, knowledge, and versatility. Proverbs 15:22 clearly states that we will have a multitude of purposes in life. As a result, we are to seek advice for each of these purposes. The scripture clearly reveals that we will be called upon to wear many hats, to multitask. Whatever area of life God leads us to, we will need education, mentors, advisers, relevant information, and God's revelation to guide us. It is worth repeating again, we make better decisions when we are informed. As believers, according to the commandments of God, we have to give ourselves the opportunity to be successful.

Proverbs 4:7–8—Wisdom is supreme; therefore get wisdom. Though it cost all you have, get understanding. Esteem her, and she will exalt you; embrace her, and she will honor you (NIV).

As we see from the word of God, believers have an obligation to understand the concepts, ideas, and skills that are required for functioning effectively in life. Believers should have a passion for learning. Even with secular education and training, God's ways are the highest priorities for the believer, and they should be applied appropriately to every life situation. Actually, the rudiment of all education has its foundation in God's word, in God's creation, and in the ongoing revelations released by Him to humanity.

Job 35:11—Who teaches more to us than to the beasts of the field and makes us wiser than the birds of the air (NIV)?

Job 37:5—God's voice thunders in marvelous ways; He does great things beyond our understanding (NIV).

The academic disciplines of the humanities, the empirical approaches of natural science, principles, technological advancements, sound enterprise, and concepts used to train humanity come from the mind, heart, and initiatives of God. We learn amazing things from the study of God's creative genius. It should come as no surprise to believers that God gives us good information and good things to meet life's necessities, and that He creates an environment that provides a comfortable existence for His creation. From God, humanity received its cognitive ability: its listening and speaking ability, its intellect, ingenuity, and wisdom. In Genesis, God establishes that everything that exists and the potential we have for advancement comes from Him. Job 37:5 says that it is God who opens our minds to things that are beyond our scope. Positive progress is related to acting upon the communication we receive from God. The power to reason, to govern, and to educate ourselves lies within the existence God created.

Problems in society arise when individuals assert their own will independent from God. Historically, mankind has a legacy of taking the things that God has provided and perverting them for sensual reasons, being led by corrupt desires and Satan. Believers should acknowledge the capability of God in all their ways, and they will have results they can be proud of.

Proverbs 3:1–6—My son, forget not My law; but let thine heart keep My commandments. For length of days, and long life, and peace, shall they add to thee. Let not mercy and truth forsake thee: bind them about thy neck; write them upon the table of thine heart. So shalt thou find favor and good understanding in the sight of God and man. Trust in the Lord with all thine heart, and lean not unto thine own understanding. In all thy ways acknowledge Him and He shall direct thy path.

These are powerful scriptures. I believe these scriptures were written by Solomon as he gave himself to the study of God's creation and the wisdom of God's word. These scriptures also reflect a conversation that God most likely had with Adam. Simply stated, I believe God said to Adam, if you follow My will, you will benefit from a long, productive, and successful life. I believe our Father has the same message for us today. The favor of God is attributed to addressing things from a position of integrity, faith, and commitment. The favor of men is brought on because they have confidence in your words and actions.

When the queen of Sheba visited Solomon, observed all his glory, and witnessed his wisdom, she was astonished at what she experienced. She was so impressed with the glory of God that was on the life of Solomon that she said:

1 Kings 10:8–9—Happy are thy men, happy are these thy servants, which stand continually before thee, and that hear thy wisdom. Blessed be the lord thy God, which delighted in thee, to set thee on the throne of Israel: because the Lord loved Israel forever, therefore made He thee king, to do judgment and justice.

The message we receive from 1 Kings 10:8–9 is that God transfers wisdom, creativity, and His Spirit through a man who is committed to allowing Him to use his life as a conduit. This is significantly beneficial to the believer. King Solomon surrendered his life to the discovery of the brilliance of God. As a result, when he discovered a truth, he had the capacity in his attitude to do the things dictated by the truth he discovered. Solomon made the commitment to allow nothing to distract him from the power of a compelling truth. As we see in this example of Solomon's life, God is able to use the mind and spirit of a submitted person in a powerful and significant way. We see this with individuals today who walk in the Spirit of God and honor the gospel of Jesus. They perform miraculous things in the lives of people by the power of the Holy Spirit that is allowed to move freely in their lives. In accordance with Psalm 1:1–3, today, believers can attain the glory of God that was present in the life of Solomon and the people under his care. As we demonstrate a life committed to wisdom, searching for truth, proceeding with understanding and integrity, and with the motive to glorify God and treat people with justice, God will use us in significant and powerful ways. God will channel greatness and immeasurable success through us that affects not only our family and circumstances; the glory will also touch the lives of others.

In the following scriptures, Job describes the effects of the blessings of the Lord on his life because of his faithful response to be active according to God's way.

Job 29:3—When His candle shined upon my head, and when by His light I walked through darkness.

Job 29:7–11—When I went out the gate through the city, when I prepared my seat in the street! The young men saw me, and hid themselves: and the aged arose, and stood up. The princes refrained talking, and laid their hand on their mouth. The nobles held their peace, and their tongue cleaved to the roof of their mouth. When the ear heard me, then it blessed me; and when the eye saw me, it gave witness to me.

Job 29:14—I put on righteousness, and it clothed me; my judgment was a robe and a diadem.

Job 29:25—I chose out their way, and sat chief, and dwelt as a king in the army, as one that comforteth the mourners.

In these scriptures, Job states that the blessings that came upon his life, the favor of God, and the favor he received from man was directly related to his decisions to treat his fellow citizens fairly, to be willing to distribute to people in need, and to be a resource of wisdom to solve the problems of his community. Because of this position, Job's wealth and possessions far exceeded all others in his region. The richness of his life was not just in monetary things and in a blessed family, but also in the wisdom he received to conduct his business affairs and the peace he received from God. Job's experience of the enduring value of the success of God is captured in the following scripture:

Job 36:11— If they obey and serve Him, they shall spend their days in prosperity, and their years in pleasures.

We need to share the passion of Job for what is said in Job 36:11. In making decisions, we are to always search for the wisdom of God. We were designed to depend upon God for direction from the beginning of time. This is a key in maximizing our potential! We can overcome the challenges and obstacles of life if we maintain a position of commitment to God's way.

Philippians 2:8—And being found in fashion as a man, He humbled Himself, and became obedient unto death, even the death of the cross.

In the Hebrew language, fashion means prepare, establish, or fix. Humanity is fearfully and wonderfully prepared in the image of God. We possess the power to send men to the moon, walk in space, split atoms, launch satellites, perform heart and brain surgery, run fast, jump high, and procreate. Even with these abilities, our position relative to God the Creator and His Son, Jesus Christ, is ultimately to humble ourselves in all situations and follow His will according to Philippians 2:8. This is the essence of the "fashion" of man. The way God has established humanity is to have daily communication with his Creator, to listen to the Creator's instructions, to do what the Creator commands, and to receive gifts from the Creator. God the Father, Jesus, and the Holy Spirit did not stop working with and advancing the thoughts of humanity after the creation of the Garden of Eden. No, the three members of the Godhead are still active in the hearts, minds, and affairs of humanity today. When believers embrace this truth, we can change our lives in the power of this knowledge.

At times during our walk with God, it seems as if He does not communicate with us. We go through situations where we look for God to talk with us and to communicate something. It appears as if He remains silent. The reality is, God is always there for us: He is a present help in the time of need. However, there are times when God wants us to use what we have learned, to use encouragement and self-motivation. When we have exhausted the limits of our ability, God will talk with us and give us the instructions we need to move forward. As believers, we have to walk in faith, knowing that God is our advocate and that He is orchestrating things for our advancement.

Make the decision to trust God and keep walking in the things that you know are of God because they will allow you to transcend your problems and achieve success. It is guaranteed by God. Take on the soliderlike mentality; keep moving forward until you reach the destination God places before you. Control your heart's desires, make the proper decisions, and sustain your success.

Chapter Six
Times and Seasons

A farmer will plant seed for a harvest understanding that the timing is right to release his seed. He will wait patiently to reap during the harvest season. The farmer understands that what is done correctly in the planting season will manifest itself in the harvest season.

Times and seasons affect the activities of a person. Certain actions are assisted (supported) in one season that are not in another. God puts into motion and supports in one season what He will not in another. His decision is based upon what is and is not appropriate for the season. Each season has a specific nature and purpose unique to itself.

Ecclesiastes 3:1—To everything there is a season, a time for every purpose under heaven.

The scripture conveys to us that time controls the occurrence of a season, that every season has an activity or purpose inherent within itself, and that God controls time. The winter and summer are seasons unlike one another, occurring at different times with different activities and purposes. The winter season brings cold weather, and the summer season brings warm weather and vacation time. It would be completely dysfunctional, unwise, and unhealthy for someone to don his or her swimwear and head for the beach with a picnic basket and a cooler full of soft drinks in the midst of winter with subfreezing temperatures and an iced-over lake. This activity would be more conducive to and supported by the summer season. As the earth is impacted by natural seasons, the believer's life is impacted by spiritual seasons.

Seasons take on the characteristics described throughout the third chapter of Ecclesiastes: seasons of gain, seasons of loss, seasons of sorrows, or seasons of laughter. Spiritual seasons designed by God are released to accomplish specific goals (purposes) in the life of the believer! It is vitally important with regard to the potential of believers to discern the season they are in to maximize the benefits of that season. With understanding the purpose of a season, complaining can be stopped, delays can be eliminated, and we can spend more time effectively moving forward in the things of God.

Seasons are powerful. Storms are also powerful. Paul's voyage from Jerusalem to Rome represented in Acts chapter 27, illustrates the power of a season and the impact that it has in the believer's life when an action is done out of season. We also see the control that God's word has on both seasons and storms.

Acts 27:10–11—And said unto them, Sirs, I perceive that this voyage will be with hurt and much damage, not only of the lading and ship, but also of our lives. Nevertheless, the centurion believed the master and the owner of the ship, more than those things that were spoken by Paul.

Acts 27:21—But after long abstinence Paul stood forth in the midst of them, and said, Sirs, ye should have hearkened unto me, and not have loosed from Crete, and to have gained this harm and loss.

In this account of Paul's voyage to Rome, we see that the sailing season would not support a voyage that had the length of Paul's journey. Sailing became dangerous on the open waters, and the wind of the Algerian sea was not blowing strong enough to permit a ship to cross. What we learn from this account of Paul's voyage is that we should not move on a thing if it is not God's will. As believers, we should always understand the season and situation that we are in and get the counsel of God and follow His lead. Paul, given the understanding of the timing of the season by the angel of God, warns the master of the ship not to set sail. However, because of the pressure of the power of Rome, Julius the centurion, who was in charge of the voyage, heeded the words of the helmsmen and owner of the ship over the objections of the word of God spoken by Paul. The men of the ship, supposing that they would be able to obtain their desire, set sail, unaware of the dangers that lie ahead. Paul knew because the angel of the Lord had warned him that danger was ahead.

Life can be as unpredictable as the Algerian Sea when we move outside of the word and season of God. Moving contrary to the permission of God will leave us to our own efforts in trying to control situations we are confronted with. God's grace, however, will be in effect. As you continue to read the account of Paul's voyage in Acts 27, we see many activities undertaken to save both the lives of the men and the ship. In these efforts, everything of value was thrown overboard, including the tackling of the ship. All that the men of the ship did to try to gain control of the vessel was useless. The power of the storm was more powerful than their efforts. In the end, the efforts of the men were not enough to offset the force of the powerful storm. We see that after many valuable things were lost, after a lot of fear and prayer, Paul stood in the midst of the ship and reminded the men what he had said days earlier. Paul informed the group of a wise kingdom principle: to obey is better than sacrifice. The damage that was suffered as a result of moving out of season was significant. If the men of the ship had listened to the advice of God that Paul communicated, the disastrous situation would have been averted.

Julius the centurion was ultimately the director of the voyage. As a Roman official, whatever Julius commanded had to be carried out. The decision of this person had a powerful effect on all. The lesson we learn here is that we have to choose carefully those who we are in relationship with, from the perspective of secular and religious relationships. The life of the believer should be surrounded by relationships appointed by God. These relationships influence where we work, live, and die. God should be allowed to be involved in all of our relationships because they have such a tremendous impact on what occurs in our lives. We see the poor results that Paul experienced because of his relationship with undiscerning men.

In the Hebrew language, a word for bond is yoke. In biblical terms, yoke is used to describe a pair or team of oxen joined together at the neck by a mechanism designed to harness the power of the oxen to accomplish a desired result. In this situation, Paul was yoked with his fellow voyagers because of their common destination, Rome. Because Paul was yoked in his relationship with the men of the ship, he had to ride out the storm someone else had created. Paul knew they should have remained in Crete, but because other men were directing the activities of the men in charge of the ship, he suffered with everyone else.

As we follow the account of Paul's voyage, we see tremendous loss. The situation finally begins to turn around only when the men of the ship learned to obey the word of God. As a result of everyone submitting to God's word and abiding in the ship according to the instructions of Paul, no life was lost. The faithfulness of God's word provided a safe haven for all 276 men on the ship. The providence of God negated the potential for death that could have resulted due to the centurion's decision. God knew the men on the ship who could not swim would use the pieces of the broken ship as flotation devices, and He also knew those who could swim would not drown in the waters of the sea. This would all happen according to the word given to Paul. All 276 voyagers arrived safely to the island of Melita.

Acts 27:24–26—and said, 'Do not be afraid, Paul. You must stand trial before Caesar; and God has graciously given you the lives of all who sail with you.' So keep up your courage, men, for I have faith in God that it will happen just as He told me. Nevertheless, we must run aground on some island" (NIV).

After three months on the island of Melita, the season to sail arrived again. This time, God permitting, the ship *Alexandria* carried Paul and the rest of the men to their destination.

Acts 28:11—And after three months we departed in a ship of Alexandria, which had wintered in the isle, whose sign was Castor and Pollux.

Thank God for people who understand the power of seasons. The men of the *Alexandria* were men of understanding and wintered their ship in a safe harbor. These men were content with the season and waited for the right time to sail again. After three months of wintering the ship, the time to set sail arrived.

Destiny seasons are powerful events in the life of the believer, just as natural seasons are upon the earth. The purposes of all seasons are given by God, both natural and spiritual seasons. Destiny seasons are particularly and specifically designed by God to prepare individuals for things that will manifest in the future. As believers, we do not pick seasons; they are guided by divine providence. Seasons enter with strength into our lives, and we respond to the power of the season according to its designed purpose. Destiny seasons are guiding influences during the life of the season. As it is with natural seasons, a season will expire and another will come. Spiritual seasons do not come with the regularity of natural seasons. Spiritual seasons are timed and released by God.

Another example of the uniqueness of seasons is displayed in the life of Joseph. When Joseph was a young lad, God gave him two dreams that indicated he would be a man of significance. However, these dreams did not materialize for many years. By the providence of God, Joseph was prepared slowly and with great care to handle the position God would create for him. Joseph had seasons of obscurity in the house of his master, Potiphar, and during the season he was the chief trustee in Pharaoh's jail. Joseph's seasons of obscurity were two progressive seasons, linked together as consecutive stages. Together, the seasons challenged Joseph and allowed him the time to mature and prepare for the very demanding job of leading a nation out of desperate conditions. Because the seasons accomplished their purpose in Joseph's life, when the season of promotion came, Joseph was ready. Scripture indicates that Joseph was thoroughly prepared by God during these seasons, and that he prospered in all that God had given him to do. In chapter nine, we will take a closer look at the life of Joseph to illustrate what God does in the life of the believer to prepare him or her for success.

Like Joseph, all believers have spiritual seasons that are arranged by God. The timing of God's seasons is predetermined by Him. If one obeys the timing of God, the things of God that are punctually determined will appear at the appointed time. To communicate His exclusive control over spiritual seasons, God asked Job in the thirty-eighth chapter of Job where he was when He laid the foundation of the earth and fixed the times of the seasons. Here, God indicates in His word that He is an independent power. He predetermines the activities and controls the preparations of man. The power that man has is to make decisions that line-up within the will, the timing, and seasons of God.

As believers, we have to be sincerely committed in following God. At times, we know that a delay of progress has occurred in our lives. The good news is that a delay is not denial. Timing is important in everything. As believers, we must recognize the timing and seasons of God to maximize results and make correct decisions. Only with revelation from God can we anticipate and prepare for future events. As God said to Abraham in Genesis 18:17, *I will not hide the thing that I will do.*

Because God controls seasons, there is a tendency for humanity to blame God for many of the negative things that happen in life. This is an ill-advised position to take. We have to separate that which is purely the act of God from that which is determined by the will of man. God is not the author of confusion. The things that are orchestrated by God produce good results. Everything that God creates and orchestrates is good. As believers, we are to simply work within the framework of the spiritual seasons of God and achieve the purpose for which the season was designed to produce. As a result, we maximize our potential to handle the responsibility God is motivated to place in our hands.

Chapter Seven
To Obey Is Better Than Sacrifice

If we are to experience the best of God, we can only accomplish this by being obedient to His word. Under the Old Testament, sacrifices were made for disobedience. To emphasize why God desires obedience, consider the following scenario. Imagine God standing before us with His word in His right hand and sacrifices in His left hand, and He presents the following situation to us: make a decision as to what you think would be the best of the choices in My hands. Obviously, the best choice would be to pick God's word because of the benefits it would bring and the suffering that it would eliminate. Choosing God's word does not cancel out the need for the forgiveness in His left hand. Thank God for this provision in our covenant relationship with Him. No one is perfect. We all need the grace and forgiveness God offers us. We need it as much as we need the air we breathe. However, nothing is more pleasing to God than total obedience. This is more acceptable to Him than anything else is.

Proverbs 21:3—To do what is right and just is more acceptable to the Lord than sacrifice (NIV).

We use our faith in doing what God asks us to do, knowing that this is the highest form of pleasing Him. Something inherently beneficial will happen for us by acting on God's word. God's original intent when He created man was to have obedience, not sacrifice. God wanted to walk in the cool of the evening with the man He had created. He wanted to welcome him warmly into His presence and to give him good things. With Adam breaking the relationship, God had to sacrifice animals so that their skins could be used to cover Adam's sin. Adam could no longer walk with God in the garden. The resulting sin brought on by Adam's disobedience was the basis of the death of Jesus. Thank God for Jesus's ministry of reconciliation. He bore our sin of disobedience; He became the lamb sacrificed to cover our sin, and He provided the way for our reinstated fellowship with God.

Hebrews 9:28—So, Christ was sacrificed once to take away the sins of many people; and He will appear a second time, not to bear sin, but to bring salvation to those who are waiting for Him (NIV).

The result of a pattern of disobedience in the life of a believer disconnects us from the flow of God's goodness: wisdom, knowledge, glory, and power. God's grace toward us is in effect during this time; however, we cannot move forward in our relationship with God until reconciliation with His will has been established. When God is satisfied that the situation has been corrected, then moving forward is permitted. What God wants us to see is the significant waste that is associated with disobedience! When disobedience takes place, forfeiture and delay of something occurs. God is not pleased with lack; He prefers us to walk in prosperity. Obedience is the preferred way to conduct our lives. Successful living is achieved in this manner. In obedience, we activate the goodness of God. Disobedience activates disappointment. The life experiences of King Saul illustrate this principle.

1 Samuel chapter 15 begins with the account of God giving King Saul a commission to go and fight with the Amalekites.

1 Samuel 15:3—Now go, attack the Amalekites and totally destroy everything that belongs to them (NIV).

The commandment of the Lord was clear. Saul was to destroy the Amalekites and everything the Amalekites owned. As you read the account of the battle, you will notice that Saul did not execute the assignment as God had instructed him to. Verse 9 of 1 Samuel

chapter 15 notes that Saul, in collusion with his soldiers, decides to

spare King Agag and the best of the livestock.

1 Samuel 15:9—But Saul and the army spared Agag and the best of the sheep and cattle, the fat calves and lambs—everything that was good. These they were unwilling to destroy completely, but everything that was despised and weak they totally destroyed (NIV).

It is clear that Saul's disobedience to God's instructions was

purely motivated by self-gain and self-glorification. As Samuel

continues to talk to Saul, he asks him what his motive was in

dismissing the instructions of God.

1 Samuel 15:19—Why did you not obey the Lord? Why did you pounce on the plunder and do evil in the eyes of the Lord (NIV)?

Saul's motive was purely covetousness. In his eyes, the financial

value of the Amalekites' animals would far exceed the value he

would receive from following the word of God. However, the

immediate gratification Saul received by increasing his wealth due

to the Amalekite livestock he spared would soon be overshadowed

by the judgment of God. Saul realized very quickly that obedience

is better than sacrifice. Here again, that old nemesis of rebellion

to the word becomes a major influence in the life of the man God

designated to use. As we look back at the fall of man in Genesis 3:6–

13, we see the same issue of disobedience to the word of God. Adam and Eve failed to follow the directions of God's word, thinking that they would gain benefit from a poor decision. Saul also fell into this same trap. Something good does not happen when a course of action is decided upon that deliberately goes contrary to the will that God has communicated to us. Saul discovered, as did Adam and Eve, that to obey is better than sacrifice.

Following this event, God rejected all attempts of Saul to be restored as king of the kingdom. Saul's attitude was one of compromise. Saul rejected the word of God and refused to do what was right, situation after situation. His rebellions prevented him from moving forward in the things of God. The matter at hand was one of obedience, and Saul failed as miserably as Adam and Eve. Because of his disobedience, Saul would be stripped of the kingdom, and it would be given to David as soon as David and the Israeli people were prepared to receive him.

As we continue to read the conversation between Saul and Samuel, you will notice Saul's defiance in acknowledging that he had done anything wrong. You can also see on numerous occasions that he attempts to vindicate his actions. At this point, Samuel stops Saul from justifying his actions and says to him:

1 Samuel 15:22—But Samuel replied: Does the Lord delight in burnt offerings and sacrifices as much as in obeying the voice of the Lord? To obey is better than sacrifice, and to heed is better than the fat of rams (NIV).

Saul did not represent any sincere repentance or any indication that he valued the word of God. If Saul would have demonstrated sincere repentance and humbleness of heart, he would have been forgiven and God would have continued to assist him as king. Saul's corrupt inclinations and opposition to the commandment of God, however, led God to replace him with David. Saul rejected being governed by the word of God. Saul allowed himself to fail the "heart assessment" test. The desires of Saul's heart became a barrier to his success with God. Everything that Saul wanted was motivated out of selfish, carnal, and sensual desires. God wants us to see that if we disrespect His word and will not allow Him to govern our activities, then we cannot govern the things that are His.

To identify clearly the covetous heart (jealous and greedy) and self-exalting behavior of Saul, look at 1 Samuel 15:12. Saul's actions were not related to a lack of understanding or instruction, or a lack of knowledge. Saul's actions resulted from a lack of wisdom and total disregard for the word of God. Here we see Samuel looking for Saul after God informed him that He rejected Saul as being king over Israel. As Samuel searches for Saul, Saul is celebrating his victory over the Amalekites. This was Saul's victory; God did not recognize it because Saul did not do as God commanded him.

1 Samuel 15:12—Early in the morning Samuel got up and went to meet Saul, but he was told, Saul has gone to Carmel. There he has set up a monument in his own honor and has turned and gone on down to Gilgal (NIV).

In searching for Saul, Samuel did not find him at Carmel. However, Samuel was informed that Saul had erected an arch of triumph commemorating "his" victory over the Amalekites. Samuel was also informed that Saul had gone from Carmel to Gilgal, and that Saul had orchestrated a parade (military victory march) for himself in celebration of his victory over the Amalekites. The parade started at Carmel and ended in Gilgal. No doubt, Saul displayed King Agag in the parade as a trophy to his glory, representing the defeat of the Amalekites. In these acts, we see the self-indulgence of Saul. When Saul should have been more concerned with the justice of God, helping the people under his leadership experience the prosperity of obedience to the word of God, Saul was preoccupied with the greed, jealousy, and self-adulation of his heart's desire. Saul was promoted to rule with justice for God, to advance the kingdom, to lead the nation with integrity, to prepare the heart of the nation for the use of their God, and to give the people an administration based on the integrity of God's word. Saul failed to control his heart and abused the power of a very important position. Saul did not honor God, because the scripture states, Saul "turned away" from following God.

1 Samuel 15:11—I am grieved that I have made Saul king, because he has turned away from Me and has not carried out My instructions (NIV).

As a result, David was chosen as Saul's successor. David was chosen because of his reputation as being a lover of God, whose heart was tender and who submitted to the word of God. From his youth, David had demonstrated charity and integrity as he managed his father's resources and the resources of God. From the account of David's life in scripture, you can see that David placed his life on the line for God and the people of God his entire life. This was David's first order of business each time God promoted him. David and his administration were geared to keep the people of God free of oppression. The Bible represents David fighting the Lord's battles, following the Lord's decrees, and pursuing the Lord's justice. The following scriptures, written by David, reveal the love he had for the

ways of the Lord.

Psalm 119:7–11—I will praise You with an upright heart as I learn Your righteous laws. I will obey Your decrees; do not utterly forsake me. How can a young man keep his way pure? By living according to Your word. I seek You with all my heart; do not let me stray from Your commands. I have hidden Your word in my heart that I might not sin against You (NIV).

When David did wrong, he had a penitent heart. Saul had an

unrepentant heart. Saul's actions were evident that God could no

longer trust him with the power He had given him.

With authority comes responsibility. We have to govern ourselves

in the ways of God. From his youth, David had the reputation of

pleasing God, of being a man after the heart of God. The character

of the heart and spirit of the person God will use is recorded in

Psalm 1:1–2. We cannot move forward in the plans and resources

of God with self-centered, self-promoting desires. The goal of the

person God uses seeks the justice of God. In 1 Samuel 18, verses

6–9, we see a further display of the condition of Saul's heart.

1 Samuel 18:6–9—When the men were returning home after David had killed the Philistine, the women came out from all the towns of Israel to meet King Saul with singing and dancing, with joyful songs and with tambourines and lutes. As they danced, they sang: Saul has slain his thousands, and David his tens of thousands. Saul was very angry; this refrain galled him. They have credited David with tens of thousands, he thought, but me with only thousands. What more can he get but the kingdom? And from that time on Saul kept a jealous eye on David (NIV).

The individual God calls to His purpose has the responsibility of seeking God's word and following God's word in every situation. God's people must have a heart that the Spirit of God is allowed to dwell in, so that He can direct their activities. Their disposition of being obedient to God does not mean that they are prefect; no one is. Our obedience to God refers to our love for Him.

Proverbs 21:1—The king's heart is in the hand of the Lord. He directs it like a watercourse wherever He pleases (NIV).

A watercourse does not determine its own flow, it simply follows the predetermined, carved path in the earth created by the hand of its designer. As a farmer channels the water where he wants and regulates its flow, so does the Lord with the heart of the king.

Job 36:22—Behold, God exalteth by His power; who teacheth like Him.

A king's decisions are under the control of God. God speaks to the king; the king receives and hides the word of God in his heart. The king embraces the words of God and uses all his strength to accomplish what God has revealed to him. As the king establishes the word of God, the word of God works to establish (exalt) the king. Likewise, as we establish the word of God in our hearts, God's word works to establish the believer. We all are designed to function in this manner toward God. God is supreme, and we willingly serve Him. The person God uses for His glory has to have the disposition of one that will totally submit to His will. God is delighted in the faithful practice of an individual willingly following His word. This enables God to influence his or her decisions and activities. Moreover, because of the influence of God on the decisions and activities of the person, the individual reaps the harvest of obedience.

Isaiah 1:19—If you are willing and obedient, you will eat the best from the land (NIV).

The scripture conveys to us that the best possible results for an individual to achieve will occur when a willing and obedient attitude is demonstrated. As we allow the word of God to be our guide in the challenges, problems, or opportunities we have to deal with or respond to, we can expect to have success in every situation.

A great example of a person with a willing and obedient attitude (spirit) was Ruth. The results Ruth received illustrate what Isaiah 1:19 teaches us.

Beginning in the first chapter of the book of Ruth, Ruth's story unfolds to us. The first chapter begins by recounting the loss of Naomi's family and the loss of Ruth's husband, Naomi's eldest son. What is interesting about the narrative is the disposition of Ruth. Ruth had faith in an unseen land, an unfamiliar God, and the words of her mother-in-law, Naomi. The narrative gives us a tale of Naomi's two daughters-in-law, both in the haze of attempting to make sense out of all that had happened to them and where they would go from there. With the future unpredictable, Naomi decides to return home, hearing that the Lord had visited His people and good things were happening. Somewhere during her association with Naomi, Ruth had developed a high regard for her faith and testimony. Being the godly woman she was, I am sure Naomi shared with her daughters-in-law the testimony of God's goodness to the children of Israel. No doubt, Naomi gave the women a full account of the trials of the Israeli people, the deliverance God gave them, and the covenant He established with them. I am sure being a part of a devoted Jewish family had a lot to do with her faith as well. In Naomi, Ruth found her life's coach, and she would stay by her side until death separated them. Note: never allow a problem to come between you and your life-coach. This relationship is far too

valuable to lose. The relationship is one God has built. No person or

situation should be allowed to dissolve this relationship. It should be

maintained at all costs.

Oprah was impacted by the loss of her husband and struggling

to understand what direction to take, just as Naomi and Ruth were.

Oprah decides on a path different from her sister-in-law's.

*Ruth 1:14–18—At this they wept again. Then Oprah kissed her
mother-in-law good-by, but Ruth clung to her. Look, said Naomi,
your sister-in-law is going back to her people and her gods. Go back
with her. But Ruth replied, do not urge me to leave you or to turn
back from you. Where you go I will go, and where you stay I will
stay. Your people will be my people and your God my God. Where
you die I will die, and there I will be buried. May the Lord deal with
me, be it ever so severely, if anything but death separates you and
me. When Naomi realized that Ruth was determined to go with her,
she stopped urging her. (NIV).*

Thank God for giving Ruth the courage, faith, and conviction to

understand that her destiny was tied to following Naomi. Ruth made

the decision to place her destiny in the hands of the God Naomi

served. The following verses give us a quick look at the character

of Ruth. She was a virtuous woman, humble, trusting, trustworthy,

industrious, graceful, and temperate. The man her destiny was tied to, Boaz, who she was about to meet, was also impressed with Ruth's character.

Ruth 2:11–12—Boaz replied, I've been told all about what you have done for your mother-in-law since the death of your husband—how you left your father and mother and your homeland and came to live with a people you did not know before. May the LORD repay you for what you have done. May you be richly rewarded by the LORD, the God of Israel, under whose wings you have come to take refuge (NIV).

Ruth's willingness to follow the word of God guided her in making a good decision. By obeying all that Naomi told her to do, in following the instructions of Boaz and maintaining a willing attitude, Ruth positioned herself to receive a tremendous reward, one that would have great significance and reach beyond her lifetime.

As we continue to read Ruth's story in the scriptures, we see that she was unaware that her decisions were guided by providence. God was working to establish her. The consistencies of her decisions led her to the parcel of land owned by Boaz. Under the covenant established by God with the Israeli people, when a male died leaving no sons to carry on the legacy of the family, the male next of kin had the obligation to care for the widow and raise up seed in the name of the departed male. To Ruth, Boaz was that man. Late one evening after having worked all day in Boaz's field, Naomi and Ruth had a discussion regarding this covenant provision. It was at this point that

they both realized what God's providence was orchestrating.

Ruth 2:19–20—Her mother-in-law asked her, where did you glean
today? Where did you work? Blessed be the man who took notice of
you! Then Ruth told her mother-in-law about the one at whose place
she had been working. The name of the man I worked with today is
Boaz, she said. The Lord bless him! Naomi said to her daughter-
in-law. He has not stopped showing His kindness to the living and
the dead. She added, that man is our close relative; he is one of our
kinsman-redeemers (NIV).

Little did Ruth realize when she made the decision to glean in

the fields of Boaz that she would become the wife of the owner of

the fields she worked in. Providence guided Ruth's footsteps to the

fields of the most probable, most able of all the kinsman-redeemers

in Bethlehem, who could redeem all that Naomi's family had lost

and provide support for both Ruth and Naomi for the rest of their

lives. The rest of the story of Ruth is history. She marries Boaz, and

they have a child who is destined to be a member of the genealogy

of Christ. Naomi's fear and frustration were replaced with joy and

happiness. The covenant of God provided support for her in her

latter years.

Ruth 4:13–17—So Boaz took Ruth, and she became his wife. Then
he went to her, and the LORD enabled her to conceive, and she gave
birth to a son. The women said to Naomi: Praise be to the LORD, who
this day has not left you without a kinsman-redeemer. May he become

famous throughout Israel! He will renew your life and sustain you in your old age. For your daughter-in-law, who loves you and who is better to you than seven sons, has given him birth. Then Naomi took the child, laid him in her lap and cared for him. The women living there said, Naomi has a son. And they named him Obed. He was the father of Jesse, the father of David (NIV).

Ruth conducted herself in a willing and obedient spirit. She could have at any time changed her mind about working in the field under a very hot sun. She could have simply made the decision that the situation was not to her liking and gone to another field to glean. Thank God she did not. Destiny directed her footsteps. As we read the account of Ruth's character, we notice that each time Naomi gave her instructions in how to handle situations, she was consistent in following her instructions diligently. In the end, the field that Ruth gleaned in became hers. Ruth received the best that the land had to offer, as the word of God recorded in Isaiah 1:19 indicates. Ruth was having her cake and eating it too. Because she was willing and obedient, she received the best the situation had to offer. Not only was she blessed as a result, she was also instrumental in restoring the blessing of the covenant to Naomi. Naomi was taken care of, and she had the pleasure of nursing the grandfather of David. Reflective in Naomi's heart was a motivation to find rest for Ruth.

Naomi informed Boaz of his covenant obligation to Ruth's deceased husband. As a result, we see an excellent ending for all involved.

God is generously motivated as it relates to the maintenance of His people. He is motivated to see that we are cared for in a liberal regard. We see this in the story of Ruth. If we make the right decisions, develop consistency in following the will and word of God, and maintain a willing and obedient attitude, we can accomplish our destiny, realize our dreams, fulfill our potential, and walk with God in peace and joy.

Isaiah 1:17—Learn to do right! Seek justice, encourage the oppressed. Defend the cause of the fatherless, plead the case of the widow (NIV).

In this verse, Isaiah underscores the authority and urgency of God's commands to His people. We are accountable to the society we live in. The prophet's words are very clear in that we have a responsibility to help challenged people who lack the sufficiency to support and defend themselves. Christian principles have their foundation in the call for social justice, to serve and protect the underprivileged, unattended, and underserved poor in society. Compassion is an essential part of Christian living, as is faith. As Christians, we have the heart of Christ, which motivates us to sacrifice to help others. This pleases the heart of God. God works through us and with us in an effort to improve the lives of the hurting. He supports our initiatives for the self-improvement, rehabilitation, restored stability, and self-confidence of the people who have been bruised by life's circumstances. Christian philanthropy helps God with blessing those that need help. These groups also have a destiny to achieve. As we work to affect their lives in a positive way, God works in our lives, to bring about success, moral clarity, and justice.

Hebrews 13:15–16—Through Jesus, therefore, let us continually offer to God a sacrifice of praise—the fruit of lips that confess His name. And do not forget to do good and to share with others, for with such sacrifices God is pleased (NIV).

As we share our resources and the goodness of God, God is pleased with these sacrifices. This is what the anointing is for, to be a blessing to others.

Psalm 107:21–22—Let them give thanks to the Lord for His unfailing love and His wonderful deeds for men. Let them sacrifice thank offerings and tell of His works with songs of joy (NIV).

As we experience the joy of the Lord for the things He does for us and gives to us, we must not forget to be a help to others. The Good Samaritan is an example of the generosity that we should demonstrate toward people in need. This is an example of the focused giving God wants us to demonstrate to people in need. God will lead us in our giving and receiving; our hearts are in His hands. He will direct our path. When we demonstrate the willing, obedient attitude that God has given us through His word and Spirit, then we create a situation where everyone achieves. We improve our destiny opportunities as well as those who we help. With this sacrifice, God is well pleased. We are empowered to move forward to do good things.

Chapter Eight
Judgment Comes from God

Most of us are familiar with the story of the Wizard of Oz. In the story, four individuals meet, and they share their various difficulties and dreams with each other. As they journey down the yellow brick road, they hear about a man who could help them overcome their challenges and receive from him the gifts they so desperately want. Collectively, they set out for a city where the wizard behind the curtain resides. To their disappointment, they discover this wizard to be a mere man, weak in faith and with more problems than they had. The story ends with all four individuals receiving the gifts they were in search of. Much to their delight, the wizard behind the curtain reveals to them that the gifts they were searching for, they already had. The Lion had courage, the Tin Man had a heart, and the Scarecrow had a brain. Dorothy, the central character in the story, finally gets her wish, and she returns home to Kansas. With their needs met, they happily live the rest of their lives.

As children of God, we were met on the road of life by the "Godhead": The Father, the Son, and the Holy Spirit. Thank God we do not have to live a life purely dependent on the subjectivity of mere humanity. As children of God, we do not stand alone in our decision-making. We stand on the word that has been passed on to us by Father God. Therefore, we can have confidence that the decisions we make are good decisions.

John 8:15–18—You judge by human standards; I pass judgment on no one. But if I do judge, My decisions are right, because I am not alone. I stand with the Father, who sent Me. In your own Law it is written that the testimony of two men is valid. I am one who testifies for Myself; My other witness is the Father, who sent Me (NIV).

We can live life on the highest level of enjoyment by observing the advice of God, and by having daily fellowship with Him. Keys to this life of enjoyment are worship, obedience, and the acknowledgment of our fallibility.

Luke 5:4–8—When He had finished speaking, He said to Simon, put out into deep water, and let down the nets for a catch. Simon answered, Master, we have worked hard all night and have not caught anything. But because You say so, I will let down the nets. When they had done so, they caught such a large number of fish that their nets began to break. So they signaled their partners in the other boat to come and help them, and they came and filled both boats so full that they began to sink. When Simon Peter saw this, he fell at Jesus' knees and said, go away from me, Lord; I am a sinful man (NIV)!

As a testament to the enjoyment we receive from God, we see in these scriptures that the communication Simon Peter received from Jesus was outstanding! Simon Peter received so much from the instructions of Jesus that he and his partners could not retain it all. Simon was both shocked and delighted. What Simon Peter and his partners received was an example of the abundant life Jesus promised to give. With fellowship and obedience, avenues of prosperity open unto us. In fellowship with God, our perspectives change; we see new things that we could not see in our own efforts. The best judgment to handle our affairs will come from the judgments in God's word.

Jesus was given this covenant of abundant life from God to pass onto us at the beginning of creation. In heaven, before the commencement of our time, Jesus received the light of God concerning all of creation: the heavens, the earth, and the fullness of both. Moreover, because Jesus received this revelation from the Father, He has the ability to give it to those that believe in Him.

John 8:12—When Jesus spoke again to the people, He said, I am the light of the world. Whoever follows Me will never walk in darkness, but will have the light of life (NIV).

Jesus's discernment of our world was not in the wisdom of man, that is, after human standards. His "testimony" (discernment) was based on all the things the Father showed Him. As we see from the account of Simon Peter's encounter with an all-knowing and all-seeing Jesus, it was better for him to let down his nets where Jesus instructed him to do. This was the second time that Simon Peter and the disciples learned by experience to acknowledge and esteem the word of their master more than their own understanding. The first occurrence was at the marriage feast in Jerusalem, according to John 2:5. During the feast, Mary, the mother of Jesus, instructed the disciples to do whatever Jesus told them to do. This was wise counsel because Jesus is the ultimate hope for all humanity. The word of Jesus is steadfast and powerful. What He says will undoubtedly manifest according to the purpose of His word. Because Simon Peter received the testimony of Jesus, he received the power of the life Jesus came to earth to present. As followers of Christ, we are in a position to receive the life-changing information that Jesus wants to share with us.

In studying Adam's life in the Garden of Eden in Genesis chapters 1 and 2, we saw that the enjoyment of God's good land was contingent on keeping God's commandments. God gave commandments to Adam. The translation of the word command in the Greek language is advice, reason, understanding, discretion, and behavior. Because of God's commandments, Adam consciously related to his environment. There is an application of life in general that we see from the life of Adam in the Garden of Eden. The application is, God not only created Adam to be a manager of the soil, He also created him to be a receiver, a giver, and a worshipper. Adam's behavior in the garden was characterized by worship, study, listening, and obeying. Adam was a priest, not merely a worker and keeper of the garden.

We are placed in environments where we need to worship God and obey Him. This is an essential aspect of the application of life that we receive from the example of Adam's life. God commanded the man who He created, and the man worshipped. As man worships God, God fellowships with him. Thus, the lines of communication with God remain open. Because God is a loving God and is motivated for the prosperity of His people, He will share with His creation keys that unlock heaven's windows of His goodness: wisdom, knowledge, glory, power, and grace.

We learn from Adam's experience in the Garden of Eden that to enjoy ourselves and our environments, man must trust God, worship God, and obey Him. The inference is that God alone knew what was and was not good for Adam, and He communicated to Adam accordingly. We also saw in Paul's voyage to Rome in Acts 27 that if man disobeys the Father, he will have to decide for himself what is expedient and effective. Usually, the results are not as effective and proficient as the results of God's word.

Following the judgments of God in opposition to mainstream beliefs, opinions, and ideas in many sectors of our society today is an undesirable prospect for some. This mainstream disposition to oppose God's ideas accounts for many of the issues we are faced with. As the Pharisees of His day challenged Jesus, the Pharisees of today challenge our words of faith because they are not worshippers.

John 8:13–15—The Pharisees challenged Him, here You are, appearing as Your own witness; Your testimony is not valid. Jesus answered, even if I testify on my own behalf, my testimony is valid, for I know where I came from and where I am going. But you have no idea where I come from or where I am going. You judge by human standards (NIV).

If we refuse to accept what God gives us, then we make the willing choice to walk in the darkness of this world. If we walk in darkness, then we impede our ability to receive the abundant life Jesus offers us because we have no judgment.

John 1:5—The light shines in the darkness, but the darkness has not understood it (NIV).

Man was not designed to live by bread alone, but by every word that comes from the mouth of God. All of heaven—Jesus, the angels, and the Holy Spirit—will not transgress the word of God. Their activities are governed by the word of God.

Luke 4:3-4—Then the devil said to Him, If You are the Son of God, order this stone to turn into a loaf [of bread]. And Jesus replied to him, It is written, Man shall not live and be sustained by (on) bread alone but by every word and expression of God (AMP).

A poor position for people designed to obey and worship God is caused by disobedience, lack of integrity, and lack of worship. It is that simple. If we ask the question, "What are important issues in today's societies?" we can point to numerous things. However, from the guiding spiritual perspectives that serve to control our actions and motives, we have to look at the lack of worship, integrity, and maintaining a strong commitment to follow the principles God the Father, Creator of heaven and earth has established. We say this because our spiritual foundation represents the fountainhead that releases either what will be correct or wrong within the conduct of humanity's behavior.

Proverbs 14:34—Uprightness and right standing with God (moral and spiritual rectitude in every area and relation) elevate a nation, but sin is a reproach to any people (AMP).

Most of our problems have their root causes in these issues. The following scriptures reveal the answer to rectify the issue of moral and spiritual conduct.

Ephesians 5:8–9—For once you were darkness, but now you are light in the Lord; walk as children of Light [lead the lives of those native-born to the Light]. For the fruit (the effect, the product) of the Light or the Spirit [consists] in every form of kindly goodness, uprightness of heart, and trueness of life (AMP).

God looks at the entire earth as the Garden of Eden. He expects His creation to respond to Him in the same manner and methodology as Adam. God gives us advice and admonishments in how to govern our affairs and improve our environment, as He did with Adam. The author of all things is consistent. He is the same today as He was yesterday, and the way He will be tomorrow. The essence of the model of perfection God created first in the garden is what He wants today: fellowship, worship, study, peace, improvement, justice, receiving, happiness, and obedience.

By the revelation of God, we walk in success. The word of God is not idle; it is active and creative. When we receive the word of God, we are receiving power from a higher level. We are awakened by the word and Spirit of God to the characteristics of the model of humanity that pleases Him.

Hebrews 4:12—For the word of God is living and active. Sharper than any double-edged sword, it penetrates even to dividing soul and spirit, joints and marrow; it judges the thoughts and attitudes of the heart (NIV).

The goodness and power in our lives largely depend upon the degree of the word and Spirit we allow to guide us. The more of the word of God we allow to direct us, the greater the results we receive. The man identified in Psalm 1:1–3 reveals this principle to us.

As worshippers, God has provided believers with a spiritual system to access, to solve difficult problems, to gain insight into the things God wants us involved in, and to deal with the problems we encounter daily.

1 Corinthians 12:1—Now about the spiritual gifts (the special endowments of supernatural energy), brethren, I do not want you to be misinformed (AMP).

1 Corinthians 12:7—But to each one is given the manifestation of the [Holy] Spirit [the evidence, the spiritual illumination of the Spirit] for good and profit (AMP).

As priests, we minister to God. We hold the things of God to be dear to us; we esteem the word and Spirit of God above all else. God's word becomes a light unto our feet. As Jesus said, if we walk in Him, we will not falter. We are sacred vessels before God, a holy nation, a royal priesthood. In our worship, we receive the presence of God. The Holy Spirit is given to strengthen and to edify the Body of Christ. We are anointed by the Holy Spirit for leadership. This is because God understands that if blind, undiscerning leaders lead blind, undiscerning followers, everybody will fall into disorder and harm. This is the reason why God raises up men and women to lead people in the proper direction.

God is concerned with the prosperity of all of humanity. This is a principle of the garden. God created the garden where the man He created could be safe, and where "all" his needs could be met. As children of God, we should be noted for our wisdom in all affairs. We should maintain an open mind toward God and study with the intent to be an instrument to help humanity progress.

Daniel 1:3–4—Then the king ordered Ashpenaz, chief of his court officials, to bring in some of the Israelites from the royal family and the nobility. Young men without any physical defect, handsome, showing aptitude for every kind of learning, well informed, quick to understand, and qualified to serve in the king's palace (NIV).

Daniel was one the individuals discussed in the preceding scriptures, and he was noted for his worship, prayer life, and his wisdom. I believe that these three things are inextricably linked together. As you pray, listen to God, and study, God gives you excellence in wisdom, understanding, excellence in ministry, promotion, and excellence in business affairs.

Daniel 2:23—I thank and praise You, O God of my fathers. You have given me wisdom and power, You have made known to me what we asked of You, You have made known to us the dream of the King (NIV).

Daniel worshipped and prayed to God three times a day. As a by-product of his worship, he received power through the counsel of God. Because he was anointed to understand matters related to earthly living, God promoted Daniel to be the leader of the King's court, not a follower.

Daniel 2:48—Then the king placed Daniel in a high position and lavished many gifts on him. He made him ruler over the entire province of Babylon and placed him in charge of all its wise men (NIV).

What a source of power we have from the heavenly kingdom. God's command to us is to rule well, seek His face daily, and receive the highest level of joy that can be experienced here on earth. Times and seasons have not changed God. Again, what God desired when He created Adam and placed him in the garden is the same thing He wants today. He wants man to enjoy the good He created, for man to trust, worship, study, listen, receive, and obey Him. The wizard that dwells behind the curtain in the Land of Oz does not have the answers to life's difficult questions; only God does. According to John 1:5, the light of God is shining. All judgment comes from God; therefore, use His judgment (light) to prepare yourself for the move of God, and to impact your environment in a positive way.

Chapter Nine
Coat of Many Colors

Never fall into the trap of looking from a distance at the success of an individual and thinking that his or her life's work or accomplishments are somehow based on a magical journey. Success is not achieved in this manner. Success is not a flashpoint and there it is. No, the truth is that success comes as a result of many sequenced steps that ultimately accumulate into a desirable conclusion.

Multiple individuals play major roles in the success of an individual. No one can achieve alone by himself or herself. Their source of strength, vitality, and intelligence comes from God and from the individuals who were instrumental in their development. The closer you look and follow the details of the makeup of a successful person, the more you will note his or her flaws and the incremental improvement that was achieved through trial, error, hard work, and heaven's opportunities! The closer you look at success in general, the less you will see of anything magical associated with it. Through the blessings of God, we move forward in life. God opens doors of opportunity for us. Our success is achieved because God makes His ability and blessings available to us. It is the favor of God that we should look to establish our lives upon.

Genesis 49:25—Because of your father's God, who helps you, because of the Almighty, who blesses you with blessings of the heavens above, blessings of the deep that lies below, blessings of the breast and womb (NIV).

The favor of God, which is typified by Joseph's "coat of many colors," demands a walk of obedience and intelligence. As we walk toward the destiny of God in obedience, we endear ourselves to God. As a result, the blessings of God are showcased in our lives in a brilliant fashion. Joseph's life, as described in the book of Genesis, gives us an example of how the favor of God was experienced by this man.

Joseph's father, Israel, loved and favored his son. Joseph was a diligent and obedient son. However, despite Joseph's favor with his father, success did not come easy to him. Actually, Joseph's progress toward his predetermined glory started in a pit.

Genesis 37:23–27—When Joseph came to his brothers, he was wearing his beautiful robe. They took it away from him. And they threw him into the well. The well was empty. There was not any water in it. Then they sat down to eat their meal. As they did, they saw some Ishmaelite traders coming from Gilead. Their camels were loaded with spices, lotion and myrrh. They were on their way to take them down to Egypt. Judah said to his brothers, "What will we gain if we kill our brother and try to cover up what we have done? Come. Let us sell him to these traders. Let us not harm him ourselves. After all, he is our brother. He is our own flesh and blood." Judah's brothers agreed with him (NIrV).

In Genesis chapter 37, Joseph's experience in the pit seems to represent a beginning that ignited a journey and a process that ultimately led Joseph from his home to the king's palace. Joseph's pit was a launching pad to a higher destination, to become the prime minister of Egypt according to the destiny dreams God gave him. There would be many situations, decisions, and difficult circumstances to handle between the pit and the palace. Joseph would be thirty years of age before he was ready to occupy the position God would create for him as prime minister of Egypt.

Genesis 41:38–40—So Pharaoh asked them, can we find anyone like this man, one in whom is the Spirit of God? Then Pharaoh said to Joseph, since God has made all this known to you, there is no one so discerning and wise as you. You shall be in charge of my palace, and all my people are to submit to your orders. Only with respect to the throne will I be greater than you (NIV).

In adherence to God's divine order, just as he was dutiful and obedient to his father, Israel, Joseph committed himself to the goals and training of God. As a result, true to His strategy for growth, God promoted Joseph to consecutive levels of higher authority and blessings. Because Joseph was committed to God's purpose, and because of the grace God gave him to endure difficult circumstances, ultimately Joseph achieved his goals. Joseph achieved rest, peace, and the vision God gave him when he was a lad. Joseph refused to compromise himself with the influences that life brought to bear on him. The favor of God and man in his life were experienced in profound ways.

We have to commit to the plan of God and wait for the manifestation of His blessings as we move forward in life. God wants us to understand that He desires to have first priority in our lives. God is superior to us. His ways are superior to our ways; His power is superior to our power; and His intellect is superior to our intellect.

Isaiah 55:8–9—For My thoughts are not your thoughts, neither are your ways My ways, declares the Lord. As the heavens are higher than the earth, so are My ways higher than your ways and My thoughts than your thoughts (NIV).

God's perspective in how to handle situations is better than our perspective. This is why He wants to be the cornerstone of our existence, to give us the best. We cannot outthink God nor improve upon His decisions. The things God does are always very good. They strengthen us, they bring enjoyment, and they add great value to our lives. Occasionally, we cannot see the benefit in God's way of doing things because our perspective is not as large, nor as developed as His perspective. While it is difficult at times to see and understand what God is doing, we have to trust what He is doing. We must apply our gifts and stay motivated. As we do these things, we will see the plans of God come to fruition.

Psalm 105:19–22—He was in prison until what he said would happen came true. The word of the Lord proved that he was right. The king of Egypt sent for Joseph and let him out of prison. The ruler of many nations set him free. He put Joseph in charge of his palace. He made him ruler over everything he owned. Joseph was in charge of teaching the princes. He taught the elders how to think and live wisely (NIrV).

We have to depend on the judgments and blessings of the Lord to make our ways prosperous. Thus, our decisions should be in alignment with His decisions.

When God envisions a plan to build something, a strategy to move a person forward, or a strategy to correct a negative situation, He takes into consideration how things will be experienced when the vision is completed. God is a progressive God. His perspective of the future is clear. He knows how we are going to get there and how much it will take to get us to our destination. God is both the author and finisher of our faith and life. God sets the goals for our lives. In the following scripture, look at what God says to David about a poor decision David had made regarding his life and his destiny.

2 Samuel 12:8—And I gave thee thy master's house, and thy master's wives into thy bosom, and gave thee the house of Israel and of Judah; and if that had been too little, I would moreover have given unto thee such and such things.

This scripture clearly reveals that it was God's will and plan for David to be king. A closer look at this situation reveals that God was displeased with David's decision and upbraided him for not following His plan. God informs David that before David began his journey to become king, He had already given forethought to the resources needed to establish David as king of Israel and Judah. The scriptures further illustrate how liberal God was in blessing David. God's displeasure with David was related to the death of Uriah. David had committed murder to cover up his sin with Bathsheba. God chides David because he went outside of His will and plan and acted in a way unnecessary and contrary to His will. What David did was not related to the plan of God. God informs David that if the things He used to establish and bless him were "too little," He would have supplied

David with more. The importance of the story is that God is generous in His giving and that we do not have to make decisions to go outside of God's plan to have our needs met. The things we need in order to accomplish God's plans were taken into consideration before God set the plans into motion. Therefore, when it is time for the manifestation of the gift to be brought forward, God will bring it forth.

Genesis 41:42–43—Then Pharaoh took his signet ring from his finger and put it on Joseph's finger. He dressed him in robes of fine linen and put a gold chain around his neck. He had him ride in a chariot as his second-in-command, and men shouted before him, Make way! Thus, he put him in charge of the whole land of Egypt (NIV).

It is clear in 2 Samuel 12:8, that whatever you need to accomplish the will of God in your life, God has already considered it. In addition, because He has considered it, you can expect it! If your decisions are in alignment with His will, provisions will manifest. The provision will come because of God's motivation to bless and establish you. Ask God faithfully, and expect to receive from Him! As 2 Samuel 12:8 promises, the "such" things you have need of for your family, career, and life will be given to you by God.

Do not minimize what you can do or who you are on this earth. You are absolutely the delight of God. You are His favorite, the apple of His eye. In His eyes, you wear the coat of many colors. Rejoice in your God. The richly ornamented robe you wear represents two things: the preferential love that the Father has for you and the rank you hold in the earth. Your coat of many colors is an indication that God is going to make you the head, a ruler to govern in His kingdom, as Joseph did in Potiphar's house and Pharaoh's palace.

GENESIS 39:2–4—THE LORD was with Joseph and he prospered, and he lived in the house of his Egyptian master. When his master saw that the LORD was with him and that the LORD gave him success in everything he did, Joseph found favor in his eyes and became his attendant. Potiphar put him in charge of his household, and he entrusted to his care everything he owned (NIV).

As Joseph's coat of many colors illustrated his preferred status with his father, Israel, so too does your coat illustrate your preferred status with Father God.

2 Samuel 22:36—You give me Your shield of victory; You stoop down to make me great (NIV).

Stay within the will of God. Let His thoughts be your thoughts, His ways your ways. Make decisions based upon your preferred status with God. God wants to promote you. He has bestowed the multiple talents of the kingdom upon you. Do not destroy your advantage with hasty, uninformed, unfocused, unnecessary decision-making. Seek God's face, read His word, hear His voice, and let Him establish you in His will.

God's plans are our life's priority. We are all under construction, and God wrote the blueprints for our lives. The decisions we make will have a significant impact on the quality of our lives. We are like Adam, created to have fellowship with God; to make good decisions and enjoy the freedom and peace of the covenant God has established with us.

If God calls for you and asks, "Adam, where are you," let your response be, "Right here Father, right where You want me to be." If you will maintain this position, God will promote you, bless you, and assign you to kingdom responsibilities. Truly, the best is yet to come!

For believers, it is critical that we understand the importance of following His plans in all situations and circumstances. God is faithful: He will do what He promises.

Deuteronomy 7:9—Know therefore that the Lord your God is God; He is the faithful God, keeping His covenant of love to a thousand generations of those who love Him and keep His commands (NIV).

Even if we struggle with the will of God in times of difficulty, when we are without vision or faith, or when we walk in disobedience, we learn the value of submitting to His will. God wants us to succeed. He has promised to bless us as we make decisions based upon fulfilling His plans. Let God's plans be your guiding light to close the door on negative circumstances and results. Use your faith and the ability God has given you to prepare yourself for future events and to prosper in your current situation. Hear what God is saying to you, be wise in His understanding, do what He says, and avoid life's ditches.

Job 36:11—If they obey and serve Him, they shall spend their days in prosperity, and their years in pleasures.